Praise for *Smart Self-Publishing*

 Kathryn Flocken-Henriquez, author

Your book was such a valuable tool. It really helped me in creating a professional and polished package. *Silhouettes: Rediscovering the Lost Art* is hot off the press and looks great!

 Jim Cox, *Midwest Book Review*

Now in a completely updated third edition, *Smart Self-Publishing* . . . is an informed and informative 'how-to' instructional manual for succeeding in the competitive word of book publishing. Individual chapters address different venues of self-publishing, including how to be professional in both literary product as well as the human element in publishing, handling the challenges of book promotion and distribution, and taking track of money matters . . . an excellent primer for anyone with a serious interest in taking the self-publishing plunge.

 Alex Moore, book review editor, *ForeWord* magazine

Authors Linda and Jim Salisbury provide practical worth and applicable information for success in self-publishing. . . .

 Jennie S. Bev, managing editor, BookReviewClub.com, and author

Smart Self-Publishing is probably the smartest book about self-publishing available in the market. I truly appreciate the exclusive information about working with book packagers and the no-nonsense promotion tips, which gives this book a competitive edge. I read this book in one sitting and will be returning over and over. (Rated Five Gold Stars!)

 Wanda Jewell, Southeast Booksellers Association

The message is that if you are going to self-publish, do it right; a message that bookstore owners know cannot be stated clearly enough.

 Steve Carlson, *Big Books From Small Presses*

Congratulations on your success with *Smart Self-Publishing*. A lot of books come out on this topic, and yours seems to have joined the select few that are widely considered to be musts for the professional libraries of new publishers.

🦉 Frances Keiser, Sagaponax Books

This is the first book I recommend to writers interested in learning about the publishing business. It clearly explains everything they need to know.

🦉 Noreen O'Brien, NonfictionReviews.com

Phenomenal reference for self-publishers. There is a wealth of information on the process and options open to the self-publisher; the hardcore information, based on first-hand experience, is well researched and clearly written by professionals within the publishing industry.

🦉 Betsy Lampé, reviewer, National Association of Independent Publishers

Smart Self-Publishing offers many insightful publishing stories, generous how-to-information, and the book, itself, is a great example of how a book should be put together. Publishing veterans Linda and Jim Salisbury provide their wisdom in another publishing bookshelf requisite.

🦉 Waldron A. McLellon, author, *Leather and Soul,* Butternut Press

It is an impressive book, beautiful on the outside, informative on the inside. It will be a valued addition to my library.

🦉 Dr. Robert Schissel, Ed.D., author, *The Art of Cooking Leftovers*

I read it cover to cover. As the sections on the many pitfalls that can (will) beset the novice author flashed past me, I swore I was reading my own biography. Where were you when I really needed you [*before* I published my first book]?

🦉 La Donna Vick, founder of www.momsnetwork.com

[*Smart Self-Publishing*] has been a great help to the novice self-published author.

🦉 *Bottom Line/Personal*

[One of] The best books on self-publishing.

🦉 Betty Wright, publisher, Rainbow Books

Smart Self-Publishing is a compendium of information. Well-organized and written for the layperson. Anyone thinking of publishing should read this book first.

Smart
Self-Publishing

An author's guide to producing a marketable book

Smart Self-Publishing

An author's guide to producing a marketable book

Third edition

Linda and Jim Salisbury

with forewords by
Betty Wright
and
Joe Sabah

Tabby House

Manufactured in the United States of America
Library of Congress Control Number: 2002075274
ISBN: 1-881539-30-X
Illustrations: Christopher Grotke
Cover design: OspreyDesign
Photo of the authors used by permission of Church Impressions LLC
All trademarks used herein are for identification only and are used without
intent to infringe on the owner's trademarks or other proprietary rights.

To the memory of Chester Baum, a wonderful editor, author and friend

Library of Congress Cataloging-in-Publication Data

Salisbury, Linda G. (Linda Grotke)
  Smart self-publishing : an author's guide to producing a marketable
book / Linda and Jim Salisbury ; with forewords by Betty Wright and Joe
Sabah. -- 3rd ed.
    p. cm.
Includes bibliographical references and index.
  ISBN 1-881539-30-X
  1. Self-publishing—United States. I. Salisbury, Jim, 1936- II. Title.
  Z285.5 .S25 2002
  070.5'93--dc21
                        2002075274

Tabby House
4429 Shady Lane
Charlotte Harbor, Florida 33980
(941) 629-7646; fax (941) 629-4270
E-mail: Publisher@TabbyHouse.com
Web site: www.tabbyhouse.com

Contents

Foreword
to the third edition

Hardly a week passes that I don't recommend *Smart Self-Publishing* to some prospective self-publisher. Why? Because Linda and Jim Salisbury, the authors, tell the unvarnished truth about publishing. Good advice is often hard to come by. And I should know, if you'll forgive the ego.

I sold my first piece of writing at the age of seventeen. My pay for that first article was a magnificent twenty-five dollars. "Yeah," I said to myself, "I can do this!"

Anyway, I progressed and sailed along writing short stories and articles for most of the top national magazines. Then, I looked up one day and discovered the magazine market was fast disappearing. "Time to shift gears," I told myself. I wrote a novel, and it was published by the Big Boys in New York. And I said to myself, "Yeah, I can do this." But writing novels quickly became akin to slave labor. No more did I talk with people. I was utterly alone, day after day, from morning to evening. I wasn't having fun. After too many years of such work, I leaned back, put my feet on the desk and thought: I'm in the wrong business. Maybe I was meant to be a—a publisher?

I picked up my last published book and examined the mechanics of it in its finished form. Yeah, well, maybe I *could* do this. In time I did publish a first book, and it was someone else's book, a how-to book, and Rainbow Books, Inc. was born.

Necessity is the mother of invention, and I had worked hard at inventing my version of publishing. Wow! Was this great or what? I was my own boss again—well, almost . . .

Reviewers, distributors, and wholesalers, buyers were somewhat like having many bosses instead of one. They were all happy to tell me where I'd gone wrong. Fortunately, I'd done right more often than wrong, and I was having fun—except I yearned to talk with other publishers like me. But how to find them . . .

There weren't many self-publishers or small presses around in the late 1970s. Then, it came to me—start an association defining this idea. Well, I did that, too, and the National Association of Independent Publishers (NAIP) was born.

With the publication of the first NAIP newsletter and its attending promotional effort, I began to find publishers around the country, folks who worked evenings filling book orders in garages and spent their days in a home office—answering the phone, taking orders, sending out review copies of books, writing letters, farming out typesetting and printing, but basically doing it all.

Dan Poynter in California, John Kremer in Iowa, Jeffrey Lant in Massachusetts—they all started as self-publishers, and what remarkable folks these were!

I learned from them. We talked on the phone occasionally and met at book events. It was a great time to be in publishing. Many published Rainbow Books and twenty-three years later, it is still a great time to be in publishing. Oh, things have changed a bit, but mostly for the better.

Take the Internet. It's a super place to explore marketing avenues, sell books, acquire almost any information you may need. It's a wonder!

Next comes print-on-demand (POD) books. POD is certainly a wonderful way in which to keep inventory out of warehouses. And book warehousing *is* expensive. However, I'm sometimes dismayed by the POD folks who print books for the novice and place a commercial for their company on the back of every book printed. The back cover of a book is one of the most important opportunities every publisher has for selling the book, and should be used for that purpose.

Finally, one must consider e-books. The major drawback here, of course, is market size—so limited that few people outside the writing community know about them. This is not to say that the "electronic reader"

won't come into its own in the future. In fact, it could happen tomorrow. But I prefer to worry about it when the odds of selling become better.

As for the rest of publishing, that's changed. If you've never done it the old-fashioned way, then you'll not rejoice in what you encounter these days in publishing. It is still hard work galore, where you must compete with books published by the Big Boys in New York. With this in mind, you can have no better friend at your fingertips than *Smart Self-Publishing*.

Betty Wright, publisher, Rainbow Books, Inc.

Foreword
to the first and second editions

It's easy to write a book. It's easy to publish a book. The hard part? Doing it right.

As the author of three books and co-owner of a small publishing house in Denver, Colorado, I speak from experience when I say that books must be properly produced. I also know that if a self-publishing author develops a marketing strategy and makes good use of available free publicity, such as becoming a guest on radio talk shows, the book can be sold profitably.

Smart Self-Publishing, by Linda and Jim Salisbury, tells the stories of successful self-publishers and provides numerous tips that will help you create a product that will sell. The Salisburys and I have seen many examples of books that were produced professionally and filled a market niche, and also, unfortunately, many that were doomed to failure because the author did not understand how to do a book right. When authors contact me about my second book, *How to Get on Radio Talk Shows All across America without Leaving Your Home or Office,* they often send copies of their books. I wish you could browse my bookshelves as you read this foreword. Most of the books are top quality—books that anyone would be proud to have their name on. Unfortunately, quite a few definitely need help—let me change that to "needed help"—*before* they went to press.

How can we tell? One way is to look at the spines. You'd think that everyone would know that the spine should always read from the top to the bottom. That's the right way. But on my shelf I find five books where the printing started at the bottom, making it not only awkward but uncomfortable to read the title. This shows that the book is the work of an amateur. You certainly want your book to look like the books produced by mainstream publishing houses!

Now, let's look at the covers. The obviously homemade books stand out on my shelves because of covers that do not look like those of mainstream publishing houses.

These books are doomed as unprofessional products, and we haven't even opened them yet! Inside we find typos, no table of contents, no index, no Library of Congress Catalog Card [Control] Number, no ISBN, no title or half-title page, poor margins, and hard-to-read type. Each of these omissions not only distracts but marks the book as "the product of an amateur." Will this affect sales? You bet!

Thank goodness help is here. Linda and Jim Salisbury have created a recipe for doing it right—the first time. Their recipe book, *Smart Self-Publishing,* now in an even more helpful edition, walks you step-by-step through the details of book publishing from production to promoting and selling your book.

If I could pass one law, it would read: "Thou shalt not even think about publishing your own book until you've read and put to use all the information in *Smart Self-Publishing.*"

This valuable book will not only save you a bundle of money—if you follow the recipe and do it right—but it can help you make a bundle of money when you are ready to sell your books.

Joe Sabah

Preface
It doesn't have to be a dark and stormy night!

Most of us writers can relate to the late Charles Schulz's Snoopy, a beloved member of the syndicated cartoon strip "Peanuts." Through the years the family beagle struggles with his novel from atop his doghouse, never getting beyond the first few sentences. But what will Snoopy do with the manuscript when he finally reaches the conclusion? Will he try to find an agent? Perhaps Lucy? Or will he make a copy of his manuscript to send to Random House or Simon & Schuster? Snoopy has name recognition, which could help him get a paw in the door, but generally it's difficult, if not impossible, for unknown authors to sell the rights to their books—especially novels or poetry—to a major publishing house.

To find out just how hard it is to have good material even read at big publishing houses, *The Weekly*, an Orlando magazine, tried an experiment. Reporter David Wilkening was fed up with reading what he considered to be bad books put out by major publishers. He wondered if any of the literary giants of the past could be published today. To test his idea, his magazine submitted Marjorie Kinnan Rawlings's Pulitzer Prize-winning novel, *The Yearling*, under a phony title, to twenty-two publishers. Most didn't even read it. All but one—a Florida publisher who recognized the book—either rejected or ignored it.

An Associated Press article[1] describing Wilkening's experiment concluded that "publishers and authors agree that things have changed since 1938 [when *The Yearling* was published]."

Elizabeth Silverthorne, Rawlings's biographer, was quoted by the Associated Press as saying, "Now it is rare for a newcomer's book to be snapped up unless it has the backing of a literary agent or a famous author. In the old days, the publishers were more independent, and they could look into quality. Now, they're concerned only with how much a book will sell." That's right. Publishing *is* a business.

Writers should not be discouraged by present publishing conditions nor should they spend their lives waiting "to be discovered." Snoopy does not want to end up outside his doghouse on a dark and stormy night with a pile of rejection slips and nothing to show for his dreams. Neither do you! If you believe in your work, you should investigate the ways to beat the system and get your book published.

One of these options is self-publishing.

What is self-publishing? Simply put, it is you taking control of your own publishing destiny by doing your book yourself. That means putting your money into the project, and then becoming actively involved in the production of the book, its marketing and distribution. It also means personally reaping the profits. Snoopy may have heard that a number of nationally selling books were first self-published by their authors. But our literary beagle has also been warned by well-meaning friends about getting involved with vanity or subsidy presses: "They can be a rip-off, and you might not get much satisfaction or many copies of your book for your money." A few first-time authors have created professional products on their own, but they are the fortunate, perhaps accidental, exceptions because beginners are usually unaware of the details of publishing. Many others are finding that it is worth investigating contracting the services of a quality book packager or other professionals.

This alternative meets the need to make the book a professional product. After all, like most writers, Snoopy has put a lot of time and work into it. He doesn't want his book to look homemade.

Sound like a familiar story? Self-publishing authors can avoid the homemade look by following the advice in books such as this one or by working with professional book packagers, or the publishing experts such as editors, typesetters, and cover designers.

A few rights-buying publishers, some independent publishers, some printers and even some one-title author/publishers, offer packaging services as a sideline to their businesses. Wise consumers will explore various options carefully, and will ask for references rather than simply trusting someone claiming expertise to handle the project. The end result *must* be professional and marketable so that you can recoup your investment and perhaps make a profit.

That's what this book is about. It is to give courage and direction to prospective self-publishers. It is written by self-publishers who eventually became publishers and book packagers for other authors. It contains a wealth of information about publishing based on advice given to us by book distributors, buyers, publishers, marketers, editors, other authors, and on our experiences. Please note that some authors mentioned in the book are not self-published, but we believe their experiences are relevant.

We've tried to make this book honest, informative, and easy to use. Throughout the text we have flagged useful tips with the pencil graphic, and true stories and publishing adventures with the typewriter symbol.

This book can be used as a guide to self-publishing by those who want to attempt it on their own, or by those who seek to have someone else create a book for them from their manuscript. It is intended to help you get started, make you aware of those things a book needs to be professional, and point you in the right direction for selling your book. It is not meant to be an encyclopedia, nor does it pretend to have all the answers.

As independent publishers and book packagers, our philosophy of self-publishing is rather simple: If you, the author, do not have enough faith in your book to consider investing in it yourself, why should you think publishing houses will put their money into it? If you feel your book is worth creating, and you can arrange the finances, do it—but do it right!

LINDA AND JIM SALISBURY

1 Ways to get published

I have concluded that the stories are worthless—UNLESS someone in commercial publishing is willing to pay for them.
—E-mail from an author looking for a publisher

Once upon a time, as the story in the introduction goes, the publishing world was quite different from what it is today. People wrote books—poetry, essays, and novels. They sent their manuscripts off to publishing houses in big cities, and agents or editors chased them down with a contract. Advances were paid and sometimes royalties followed. Unknown authors—if they were any good—had a chance. The publishing industry has changed dramatically, though, and yesterday's publishing success story is usually today's fairy tale.

This does not mean that writers won't be able to find outlets for their books. Certainly some will be purchased by rights-buying houses, but most will not. This book is written for the latter group. Their success story may well be found in self-publishing—especially if the actual work of publishing is done properly by the author, possibly using the services of professionals.

Many writers raised on the "fairy tale" need further convincing. They have been charmed by the old publishing mystique: If a publisher won't buy my book, it isn't any good. This self-defeating spell keeps those writers from the satisfaction of having their manuscripts turned into books. It is, in fact, the ultimate vanity of publishing!

While the authors who still believe in this myth are living in fantasyland, many others are successfully self-publishing.

Why are writers driven to find someone else to buy rights to their book in order to have their work validated? Compare this way of thinking with that of any other independent creative group: artists, musicians, and photographers. Most artists purchase their own supplies, rent studio space, and cooperatively or independently show their work in galleries. They are looking for sales and good reviews, yes. But they paint, play music, or invest in their work regardless of grants or patronage. Why should books and literature be different from paintings or sculpture?

The doers have their books in hand and, if the books are produced properly, no one should be able to tell the difference between an author/publisher-produced book and one done by a major publishing house. In fact, sometimes the self-published books are better.

Publishers Weekly repeatedly underscores the problems in the present publishing market at the big houses. Nora Rawlinson, editor-in-chief, writes: "Publishing has always had to deal with the uncomfortable tension between art and commerce and has often had to leave to posterity—in the form of backlist sales [those books that have old copyright dates and are relegated to the back section of a sales catalog]—the final choice on what works over the long haul."

She continues: "It has been a common complaint among booksellers for years that there are simply too many books, which means that a book's shelf life continually shrinks. This has led to discussion within the industry about the need to publish fewer titles, so that each book receives the attention it requires to find its audience."[2]

There are several reasons for the shift from the old days of publishing to the new, but the overriding cause is money. Publishing is big business and there is an increasing emphasis on viewing books as *products* in competition with other products, rather than as literature for literature's sake. It's hard for writers to accept the fact that their book is a product on which publishing houses must be able to make a return on their investment. But that is the situation and you should want the same results with your product—your book. If you don't, then perhaps you should consider printing only enough copies to give away to your family and friends.

It takes money to produce the product. It takes money to advertise the product—lots of money on the national level, perhaps hundreds of thousands of dollars per title. Even nationally known writers need the boost of marketing hype. The cover of *Publishers Weekly*[3] trumpets:

> KING OF THE SEASON.
> Stephen King roars into Fall with two new titles
> backed by a multimillion-dollar marketing campaign.

It is very difficult for small presses to compete with this kind of blitz. Experienced book promoters who arrange author tours and television interviews tell us it is difficult, if not impossible, to work for an author or publisher with a promotion budget of less than $10,000.

Small publishers refer to the major national publishers as the "Big Guys." The large publishing houses, many themselves owned by larger companies (Bigger Guys), want a fast return on their investment, so they look for hot topics or hot authors, or authors they can make hot. They are unwilling to invest in risky projects. Frankly, it doesn't matter how good an author's material is. It doesn't matter that friends and acquaintances are truly sincere when they tell writers that they think they should be published. If the material does not fit into a publishing house's marketing line, the publisher will not buy it. Realistically, most unknown writers do not fit the needs of the Big Guys.

In *The Business of Books: How International Conglomerates Took Over Publishing and Changed the Way We Read* (Verso, 2001), author André Schiffrin notes that "five major conglomerates control 80 percent of American book sales. In 1999, the top twenty publishers accounted for 93 percent of the sales and the ten largest had 75 percent of the revenues." Schiffrin, the former publisher at Pantheon said that publishing has changed from family-owned companies to those owned by a handful of conglomerates. Today's owners are only interested in making money, and as much of it as possible.

Competition is stiff for authors seeking publishers. The reading market is increasingly limited, as people use electronic technology, the Internet, and television for information and recreation.

There is a terrific market for regional books. People visiting or living in a particular area will buy books about it. Think of tailoring your material to a geographic region in order to capture that market (see chapter 3).

Writers become discouraged when they find that New York City publishers aren't interested in reading, let alone buying, material by unknown writers, especially fiction, poetry, or children's picture books, which is, unfortunately, what most first-time authors have been busy writing.

In 1995, a front-page article in the *New York Times*[4] pointed to the growing success of self-publishers, thanks to desktop publishing. In the last ten years, the "number of new small publishers has increased by more than 200 percent, to a record 5,514 last year." In just seven years, Andrew Grabois, senior director for publisher relations for R. R. Bowker reported in an April 2002 press release that in 2001 the number of new titles had reached an all-time high—more than 135,000 books from about 70,000 U. S. publishers He said there was a "staggering" 20 percent increase in titles in one year.

A California writer sold his book, which dealt with how to make TV commercials, to a major publisher a few years ago. He received a $5,000 advance, but he is frustrated because there is no book.

Someone at the publishing house decided against taking the book beyond the acquisition stage. Perhaps the topic was deemed no longer hot; perhaps another publisher put out a similar book. All the author knows is that he worked hard, sold his rights, and probably will never see his book in print—unless he gets his rights back and self-publishes. He is not alone in this experience.

That's tough competition, especially for new writers without a publishing record and without a surefire marketing program. And now, with the addition of print-on-demand technology, it is causing changes in how the books of single-title authors are being accepted in the wholesale/distribution network.

Ann Rust, a writer of Florida historical fiction, sent out a dozen queries, but while waiting for responses began looking into self-publishing. She then took control. Her husband said he would serve as editor, and together they started their own publishing house, Amaro Books, which has published eight of her novels.

Ann works hard to sell her books. Hardly a week goes by that she is not doing a book signing or appearing on local talk shows as part of her marketing campaign. Her books are in libraries and bookstores throughout the region and are thoroughly enjoyed by readers who like a fast-paced, fun-read, while being educated about early Florida life. The profits fund her new projects and reprints.

Even when a publisher purchases material from a writer, there is still no guarantee that the book will ever be produced—even if the author has received an advance.

Maintaining control

Many authors self-publish because they want to maintain total control over their product or because they want to maximize their profits. Although we certainly recommend listening to editing and packaging experts if you want a professional product, author control and involvement can be an important issue.

Jim Robertson self-published a national, award-winning book on the history of public television. Robertson, who used a book packaging service, notes that editing control is very important. He had originally submitted his manuscript to a publishing company that had very different views on what was happening in public television programming. "I think editors can easily pervert the author's intended meaning if they are not careful," he said. "Author involvement can keep that from happening."

Control means that you have input in decisions regarding the text, cover, and title. Control means that the book will actually be produced, rather than be left on the shelf in the office of a rights-buying publisher. Control means that a self-publishing author will make the marketing decisions. A celebrity who self-publishes an autobiography can decide how and when to make personal appearances, because it is his or her money backing the book. There is no pressure from rights-buying publishers to go on a media tour to help them sell the book in which they have invested.

Self-publishing is gaining respect

Professionally produced self-published books can demonstrate their market appeal and sometimes can be sold to book clubs or to rights-buying publishers after the first printing. Self-publishing gets your book into the bookstores and in the marketplace where it can prove itself. Agents and representatives of the Big Guys are always on the lookout for successful self-published books that they can consider for purchase.

Consider the success of *The Christmas Box* by Richard Paul Evans. According to an article by Lawrence Van Gelder in the *New York Times,*[5] Evans wrote the story for his family and had twenty copies printed by a local printer. By February the following year, people were asking for it in bookstores. He then sent the book to regional publishers,

Denny Moore and his wife, Velda, set sail one day from Chesapeake Bay and ended up traveling around the world. Moore self-published the story of their adventures in *Gentlemen Never Sail to Weather* (Prospector Press), which was chosen by the Book-of-the-Month Club as an alternate selection. By 2001, 27,000 copies had been sold. He has already published two more books, *Alaska's Lost Frontier* and *The Sequel to Our Accidental Odyssey—Hundreds of practical tips, tricks and warnings; stuff every sailor should know. The Sequel* answers questions that people asked during his talks about the trip.

where it was rejected. Finally he decided to publish the story himself. As readers bought more and more copies, Evans eventually sold to Simon & Schuster, and by December, the book was in the No. 2 position on the *Times'* best-seller list and sales approached 400,000 copies. It has been just as popular in subsequent years.

Of course, not every self-published book will have such a fortunate public reception and national success. Evans obviously had a Christmas story that appealed to readers—and he was willing to invest in his product.

Or take the story of Aliske Webb's book, *Twelve Golden Threads: Lessons for Successful Living from Grama's Quilt.* According to *Publishers Weekly,*[6] Webb had been rejected by 150 publishers to which she had submitted the book. She and her husband decided to self-publish and sold the initial press run of 3,000 copies at quilt shows. She hit a market niche and sold 25,000 copies in less than three years. When the book was purchased by HarperCollins, the initial printing was 62,000 copies.

Other authors who have self-published their books and ended up with sales to a major publishing house include Margaret Atwood (a book of poetry), H. Jackson Brown, *Life's Little Instruction Book,* Pat Conroy, Deepak Chopra, and Tom Peters, among many others.

Many other self-publishers (also referred to in the publishing world as author/publishers or self-publishing authors) have watched their books receive national attention after first demonstrating salability in smaller markets. Jo Whatley Cheatham was invited to appear on the "Today Show" to discuss her book *Homecare: The Best! How to Get It, Give It, and Live with It.* Denny Fried's *Memoirs of a Papillon*: *The Canine Guide to Living with Humans without Going Mad*, coauthored by his dog, Genevieve, has received terrific national reviews and was accepted for national distribution in a pet store chain. That's not all. Little more than a year after the book's release, radio commentator Paul Harvey talked up the book on his syndicated show, significantly boosting the book's standing with Amazon.com, and the producer of "The Tonight Show" called for a review copy and video of TV interviews that Fried and Genevieve have done.

Two other self-published books that have had enough success to gain national attention and sale to a larger publishing house are Beth Fowler's *Could You Love Me Like My Dog?* and *Could You Love Me Like My Cat?* According to *Publishers Weekly,*[7] Fowler's books were successful in her home state, Texas, largely through her own promotional efforts (including selling books out of her pickup truck at rodeos). Her success caught the attention of Simon & Schuster. Her books were republished under that imprint.

The key to successful self-publishing is to make quality the absolute top priority. Quality should guide every decision in the preparation and production of the book. There is no reason that a self-published book should look homemade unless the self-publisher creates it that way through lack of knowledge or by misplaced thrift. An experienced book packager or carefully selected professionals can provide the type of direction that is needed to guide the publishing process so that doesn't happen.

Writers who want to see if their manuscript can be sold to a rights-buying publisher should send queries to those publishers who deal in the type of book they have written. In other words, send mysteries to publishers that primarily publish mysteries rather than sending copies to every publishing house listed in *Writer's Market*. Research the small presses to see which ones have specialties that might dovetail with your material. The easiest way to do this is to go to a bookstore or library and make a list of publishers of the type of material you have written. Or read book trade magazines such as *Publishers Weekly, ForeWord* or *Independent Publisher Online* or newsletters from publishers' associations (see appendix B). By so doing, you will be able to compile data about niche publishers that specialize in specific topics, such as science fiction, romance, and westerns.

Agents

We are reluctant to say much about working with agents because we haven't needed one. However, self-publishers and authors who come to our seminars on publishing have few success stories about agents to share. Many unknown authors have had their manuscripts with agents for several years and then finally decide if they are ever going to see their book in print, they better do it themselves.

In some instances you can find an agent who will do the legwork to help find a publisher that will purchase your manuscript. Increasingly, though, agents are requiring up-front fees for their efforts rather than a fee contingent upon the sale of your book, a practice that may well reduce the incentive to sell your book. Some agents handle only certain types of books, such as action and adventure, while others specialize in selling subsidiary rights for any already-published author to magazines, other publishers, large-print editions, or foreign rights.

Agents who are successful in selling materials must maintain their reputation. They will only represent books that they feel they have a reasonable chance of selling, and that means one that is edited and without glaring errors. Unscrupulous ones will live off the client fees regardless of sales.

Marilyn and Tom Ross, founders of the Small Publishers Association of North America (SPAN) suggest a way for you to get an agent or publisher to look at your material is to first self-publish with quality then "Sell the heck out of it. Establish a track record. Then approach an agent or publisher. The result will be the difference between night and day."[8]

Vanity press

Through the years, vanity press has given self-publishing a negative image. Vanity press implies that authors are self-publishing for egotistical reasons—out of vanity—and maybe sometimes they are. That is not necessarily bad, if the project is done well.

Unfortunately, a number of authors who have been rejected for various reasons by the Big Guys subsequently have been seduced and ripped off by what is known as a "vanity press." The bottom line is that authors usually pay more—as much as triple what it might have cost to produce the book themselves or by using the services of a quality book packager. And, usually, the authors relinquish the rights to their work, sometimes for two years, while the vanity press "markets" the book.

Authors may receive thirty, fifty, or perhaps one hundred copies of their book as part of the contract, and then must *purchase*

 If you are thinking of using a subsidy press, Ask your local bookstores and libraries if they receive catalogs from subsidy presses and if they order from them. Find out if the books published by subsidy presses are properly credentialed (see chapter 4). Be sure you will get the marketing they promise.

additional copies from the vanity press "publisher." The rest of the books vanish—if they were ever printed at all. They are rarely effectively marketed or sold in bookstores, except in discount (remainder) bins. The vanity press may even use the author-paid-for copies as sample books to attract more potential clients. We have had authors tell us, with some embarrassment, that they have paid $18,000 or $20,000 to have their books published by a vanity press, and have ended up with only one hundred or fewer copies for their own use. Do the math. It is hard to recoup your investment if you have only one hundred copies to sell on your own, which in effect cost *two hundred dollars each*—and the "publisher" is not really marketing the rest of the copies.

Subsidy press

Simply put, *subsidy* means that the author pays to be published. There is a distinct difference between paying to have your book produced by a book packager or having it "co-published" by a subsidy press (a variation on the theme of vanity). A book packager works for you, much as you might hire a contractor to work for you when you build a house. And, when you work with a reputable book packager you will have your own imprint and ISBN. All the rights to the book will be yours. Subsidy presses usually will apply their ISBN to your work. Sometimes they will also claim the copyright. This is also true of a number of the e-publishing sites.

It is essential for anyone considering using a vanity or subsidy press, e-publisher, book packager, or printer to be a careful consumer and not be misled by promises. We have talked to many authors whose egos are being stroked by clever marketing approaches. A subsidy press often will rave over the author's work, and tell the author that, as publisher, it will contribute *half the production and the marketing costs* if the author will contribute the other half, or that it will do the marketing if the author pays for production. Again, the author, who has paid for the entire press run, usually receives only a small percentage of the press run and must purchase additional copies from the subsidy publisher. Oddly enough, the author who is a good consumer and does some shopping around probably will discover that the amount he or she is expected to contribute to the project is actually *more* than what it would cost to have the book produced correctly by a reputable packager or by using a team of experts.

Sometimes the author will be promised a "royalty" based on a percentage after a certain number of copies are sold. Rarely does that occur. The promised marketing is usually an "extra," and can be quite pricey. The subsidy press usually offers to list the book in its catalog or to send out some press releases or fliers. These catalogs typically do not generate many, if any, sales and the author could easily do his or her own press release. In fact, authors are likely to do a better job at publicizing their books.

There are many variations on these themes, but the essence—that the author spends a lot of money and doesn't get much in return—is always the same.

In fairness, anyone thoroughly reading the promotional material and contracts from most vanity and subsidy presses will see that these companies are very careful to offer disclaimers for the sales potential of a book, and some specify marketing "opportunities" at extra cost. They are also forthright about the fact that you, the author, are responsible for subsidizing the project, and in return will receive forty percent of the retail price of any books sold as compensation, *if* any copies of the book are sold. Several brochures we have examined from subsidy presses also make it clear that an unknown author is a hard sell and that the subsidy press's marketing efforts are limited to press releases and catalogs. This information is couched between enthusiastic testimonials that imply that subsidy or vanity presses successfully market and sell books.

One such press release says that it promotes the sale of its books by telephone, correspondence, direct mail, catalogs, and by the authors themselves. When authors sign on with a vanity or subsidy press they don't realize how useless most of the promised "marketing" will be. They've been sold on the "vanity" of someone else taking on the

We know of a bookstore owner who was so convinced that a local author would produce a national best-seller that he helped finance the book. Unfortunately the bookseller provided only money, not expertise, and the production of the book was a disaster. The amateurish cover was the least of its problems. The text was not well edited and the book was not typeset. During the printing process, ink from the plates got on the rollers and pages were superimposed. Instead of having a salable product, the store owner ended up hiding the cartons of books in his storage room. This may be an extreme case of bad production, but it certainly is a caution for you to see that your product is produced properly.

responsibility for sales. But what good are worthless press releases— ones that are nonspecific or go to the wrong person at a newspaper? What good is it to have your book listed in a vanity press's catalog or fliers if bookstores or libraries do not order books from publishers' brochures, fliers, or catalogs?

A generic press release from a nationally known vanity press reads: "Dear Book Review Editor: We are enclosing a copy of a new [name of vanity press] publication by a local author. We believe that a review or feature article would be of particular interest to your readers since the author is a local resident. If you would like to interview the author, please let us know and we will be happy to assist you in making the necessary arrangements. . . ." Notice what is missing? Everything pertinent: the author's name, the title of the book and information about it—even the author's phone number. The review copy (paid for by the author) and postage has been wasted. Into the trash or giveaway pile goes the "review" copy. Meanwhile, the author believes his book is being promoted by his "publisher."

Authors should compare the following when getting bids or estimates from various types of presses: the number of actual copies to be received; the quality of the product and success of whatever marketing is part of the promise, and the amount of control that the author has in the project. Ask the salesperson for samples and references.

E-books and e-publishing

The Internet has opened up new avenues for authors to be published at relatively low cost through e-books, often available one copy at a time in a printed form, or as a download from the e-publishing site. However, the same caveat applies to these new opportunities as to the more traditional publishing venues. There are legitimate e-publishers, often focusing on a particular niche, such as mystery or romance, who buy manuscripts, edit them professionally, and pay royalties. There are many others that are neither legitimate nor professional and will rip you off. Be a good consumer. There are some major sites, such as XLibris and 1stBooks, that deal with self-publishers, and charge you for publication—starting at a few hundred dollars. XLibris applies one of its ISBNs to your work, then calls the money that it pays you for selling copies of books you have paid them to publish "royalties."

Most Internet book publishing sites do not routinely edit or proofread books so that, unfortunately, many are printed as written. They are sloppy and unprofessional. 1stBooks Library notes that it "does not edit manuscripts. You, as the author and publisher have the right (and responsibility) to decide the exact content of your book." However, it offers a list of "screened" editors and their charges. Many authors who are looking for cut-rate publishing options will forgo the expense of professional editing and instead make the book available as written. That is misplaced thrift.

If you decide to try electronic self-publishing it is important to learn all you can about how well e-books sell in retail stores, even if they are available through a wholesaler or on-line. Ask store managers how often such books are ordered. Do they order one copy at a time on request or as a special order for a book signing. Do stores stock books from e-publishers? Get samples so you can evaluate quality. Contact e-authors to get their views and recommendations. Find out who holds the book's copyright and the rights to reprint.

Printers are not publishers

So, why not just take your book to a local printer or an e-publishing site that prints out one copy at a time or allows readers to download your book? Because, printers are *not* publishers. Printing is just one part of the publishing process. Printers usually do not edit your work for grammar and style. And, they do not issue the credentials your book needs to be accepted in the marketplace. Only publishers can do that. Most printers print the copy they are given just as it is given to them. If you give them camera-ready copy and it is of poor quality, is smudged, or if the pages are not aligned, or if you have typed your book rather than had it typeset, your book will be printed that way.

Printers may not recognize that you have your book title upside down on the spine or that you should have text, bar code, price and ISBN printed on the back cover. Printers also are usually not aware of book style. Some may be able to typeset your pages, but, typesetting as such does not guarantee it will be done in proper book design, and often printers are out of their element when it comes to creating a professional book. We have seen many examples of books printed and bound by printers and most of them lack the professional look. Does that make a difference? You bet! That is, if you want to be able to sell your book rather than just give it away to relatives and friends. A home-made or poor-quality appearance can doom even the finest piece of writing. Unless a manuscript needs extensive editing or rewriting, much of the cost of producing a book is in the cover design, page formatting, typesetting, and the printing and binding. It is important to produce your book professionally, even if it costs more.

Ron Watson, a book buyer at Ingram Books, one of the nation's largest wholesalers, notes that Ingram will not handle a book that doesn't have a proper cover and credentials, including a bar code. These issues are of no concern to a small printer.

Book manufacturers are also referred to as printers; that is the nub of their business—to print and bind many kinds of books. They usually make sure all aspects of the job are done properly. Reputable firms will identify problems that you may not have noticed.

Book packaging

That brings us to book packaging or book producing. A book packager has the expertise of a publisher but works for you rather than buying or taking the rights to your book. Except under certain conditions, your packager should advise and assist you in obtaining the credentials (ISBN, Library of Congress Control Number and copyright) for your book in the name of your own publishing imprint.

Some companies specialize in book packaging. A few rights-buying publishers, some independent publishers, some printers, and even some one-title author/publishers, distributors, and others advertise packaging services as a sideline to their businesses. As a good consumer, you need to explore all your options. Ask for samples of books the packager has produced, and references and discuss the range of services that are available to you. Costs will vary tremendously based on what your book needs, such as editing or indexing, and special features you may choose, such as the type of cover or paper stock. You may get a cheaper bid from a "cookie-cutter" packager that offers only limited options than from someone who tailors an estimate to your project.

A book packager acts as a contractor to build your book. The copyright should be yours. The book should be fully credentialed in your name and should be carefully designed. You should be involved in decisions about the cover, the design, the paper stock, the editing, the size of the press run, and the retail price. And most important, you should receive *all the copies called for in your contract*—all of them! You are the one risking the money, so you should be the person to receive and control the product. And, if you are willing to do the work to market and sell your book, you will reap the ultimate profit.

Unfortunately, as the self-publishing and independent publishing field has grown in recent years, so have the number of companies and individuals who claim to be book packagers. Some do an excellent job, but we are seeing many more poor quality productions. Just because a packager can do a better job than you doesn't mean the work will be up to trade standards.

Financing your book

Do not spend money that is essential to your family's security on your book. Publishing is a risky business and there are no guarantees that you will get rich or even get your money back, even if you have a great idea and a well-produced product. Hold off on your project or try to find a backer if the risk could mean financial disaster for you or your family.

Some self-publishers have personal resources to invest in their product; others find financial backers. The backer may be a relative or friend, or, if it is a biography, even the person who is the subject of the book, or the money may come in the form of a grant from an organization or foundation. Consider approaching an outside party to help with

Linda Larsen, author of *True Power: Get It, Use It, Share It: Ten smart strategies to get what you want out of life* relates how she found financing for her book.

"Since I had decided to self-publish I contacted a book packager who gave me a good price on putting everything together for me. It was a good price—however, it was not a sum of money that I could immediately put my hands on without going into savings or liquidating an asset. I had never let not having the money stop me from doing what I wanted in the past and I wasn't about to start now. I made the decision to find a backer.

"I began to mention the project to several people. I never made a request, I just started placing the intention out in the world. I let my excitement about the project speak for itself. Within a week of making the decision to find a backer, and with only one chapter of the book actually written, I met a young man named Chris. Within a minute of meeting him, I knew he was an outstanding individual. I liked him immediately. We had not been together more than a short time when the subject turned to my book. I said that I was excited about the project and that I was looking for a backer to provide 'x' dollars.

"As I said the words, I knew what his response was going to be. I knew he was going to offer his support. When I finished my statement, he commented without any hesitation whatsoever, 'I'll back you. When do you need a check?' I could hardly contain my excitement."

The backing enabled her to have *True Power* professionally produced for sale when she is a keynote speaker at conventions and seminars, and in the retail market.

the financing for a share of the profits. For example, if you have written about caring for a child who has suffered a head injury, or if you have an unusual cancer treatment story, research or social organizations might help offset your costs. Having their name on the book also may help increase your sales and establish credibility.

Or you may be able to customize and sell part of your press run to a related corporation or business. Dr. Michael Hunter, a radiology oncologist, was able to sell 20,000 additional copies of *The Little Book of Breast Cancer* to a major pharmaceutical company, for example, within just a few months of the book's publication. Rick Fisher, author of *Mastering Math Essentials*, in addition to reprinting his popular teaching method (more than 20,000 copies in print in less than two years), has licensed the use of the book in several school systems. The districts reproduce the workbook on their own equipment and pay him a royalty for each copy. He has also completed a companion book for the lower grades. Both versions offer a proven system of teaching math that motivates students and requires only twenty minutes per day of review and exercises. Fisher's method has demonstrated dramatic results in schools, at home, and through homeschooling.

Author Mary Ereth has found backers for two books on animals, *CJ: The Guide Dog Puppy* (published by the Southwest Guide Dogs, Inc., and *A New Leash on Life* (published by the Animal Welfare League of Charlotte County). Each backer/publisher, not Ereth, receives benefit from the proceeds, and she has the satisfaction of seeing her books in print.

Stephen J. Kerr, president of Business Marketing Consultants has this to say: "Many publishers still believe that all they have to do is produce good works of artistic or literary merit and they are assured a place in the Valhalla of the publishing industry. Please review the four tires that will flatten you on the road to Valhalla: poor planning, undercapitalization, narrow vision, and naive optimism. Only proper planning, strong financing, a broad vision, and pragmatic thinking will carry you and your company up into the top. You can choose to be one of the survivors or road kill."[9]

2 Working with professionals

Harried authors may find it worthwhile to farm out production to a pro. . . . Such consultants {packagers} are different from vanity publishers. Book consultants work for a pre-set fee; profits are yours.
—U. S. News & World Report[10]

To give your book its best chance at success, you must create a professional product. Few authors are also excellent illustrators, cover designers, typographers, or able to objectively edit their own work. It is important to seek and use professionals to help you turn your manuscript into a polished book that will compete in the marketplace with those published by the Big Guys.

For your first book, you may want to find a reputable, ethical, and professional book packager or book producer to act as a contractor on your behalf—someone you will pay to deal with all the subcontractors for you—the cover designers, indexers, editors, and book manufacturers. The resource list in the back of this book provides some names in these categories, but there are many other professionals.

Book packaging

As self-publishing has become a major part of the publishing business, the number of book packagers or publishing companies that will produce books for self-publishers has also increased. Some are excellent and deliver a quality product. Others are charlatans who are happy to take advantage of your inexperience. Often authors thinking about self-publishing may ask another self-published author to help them with their book. That is fine if Author Al has created a professional product and didn't simply create camera-ready copy from a desktop publishing program and design his own cover. Author Al's ability to help Author Babs is limited to his own production experience—and novice Babs doesn't realize that Al doesn't have a bar code or an ISBN. And she doesn't realize that Al has no idea how to edit for book style or even the good sense to run spell check.

Or, Author Carl may have a quality product because a professional book packager handled the details, did careful editing and fact checking, which saved the book from disaster. Carl puts himself out as a packager based on the finished product that someone else prepared. Babs, impressed, gets suckered into hiring Carl at high cost.

Some inexperienced and unprofessional "packagers" may offer bargain-basement prices and pooh-pooh the need for a professional cover designer. One such "professional," *the author of a book on self-publishing,* suggests saving money by hiring students at art schools to design your cover. Cover design involves a specialized type of graphic artist. You may indeed find such a specialist who is new to the field, but beware: a bargain price may buy you an unsalable book. Graphic designers, even good ones, are not necessarily book cover designers.

Your initial contact with a book packager, either by phone, mail, personal meeting, or even on the Internet, should allow you to get an idea of the company's philosophy and range of services, possible costs, and estimated production time. You should ask for a list of references as well as a list of books that the packager has produced. Ask to see production samples of the company's work. After you have reviewed the information, make an appointment to discuss your project in detail. Ideally this should be a personal meeting, but if that is impossible, prepare a list of questions and use the telephone, fax, or e-mail. It is possible to work effectively long distance.

While you probably want to know what your book will cost to produce, be careful about trying to pin the packager down to a detailed figure at this early stage. There is so much variation in the costs of book production that it is difficult to generalize estimates. It's like going to a real estate agent and saying, "Tell me what a house costs." There are many variables in houses and books that determine the range of prices. Some books have a hardcover with enamel paper and hundreds of color photographs. Others have a softcover with no artwork. Others may include complicated typesetting, such as the creation of tables, charts, or long division problems.

Your packager should ask for detailed information about your material and may request sample pages to determine how much editing or rewriting may be involved. You should have general discussions about the possible appearance of the book: the best size, type of cover, the kind of paper, possible typefaces (including appropriate size), whether to use photographs or art, color or black and white, and other details. You should also discuss your thoughts about the size of the press run and the retail price of the book if it is to be sold through the book trade.

Beware of subsidy presses, editors, or packagers who try to convince you to invest in a large press run. We have talked with a number of unknown self-publishers who were advised to print 5,000 to 10,000 copies of their personal memoirs or philosophy, when 100 to 500 copies was much more realistic for the book's market. We find that an average first printing for a self-published author is 3,000 copies.

Once all the details of your project are factored in, the company should be able to give you an accurate estimate tailored to your book— a figure that obviously will change if you decide to add or remove pages, change the number of photographs, the dimensions of the book, or the press run.

Some packagers (really printers) will give you a flat figure for producing your book based on a set cost per page for one thousand, two thousand, or more copies. Typically the fee will cover only typesetting, printing, and binding, plus a choice of one or two standardized cover designs. It may or may not include credentialing. This arrangement may work to some authors' advantage and not to others, depending on the condition of the manuscript and the amount of work involved.

Books need varying amounts of developing. Usually the flat, per-page fee includes using computer spell checking, but won't include the line editing or rewriting that many manuscripts need, especially those written by first-time authors. Find out what you will get for a flat fee and what will constitute an extra charge.

A good packager will not just take your manuscript and say, "How nice," and print it. Good packaging includes editorial and design counseling as well as book production. The availability of good editing is one of the major services that may separate the professional packagers from the vanity and subsidy presses.

A first-class book packager should do the same job that a rights-buying publisher would do—namely, produce a quality product.

Beware of false experts

False experts come in many shapes and forms. They may offer free advice or charge you bundles, but they will lead you out of the mainstream, which is where you want to be, especially for your first book. False experts may be editors, artists, cover designers, packagers, or even proofreaders. Sometimes they are authors or seminar speakers. They are often people who mean well, but can easily lead you astray because they don't understand the publishing field, marketing, book style, or what a professionally produced book should look like.

Let us use graphic artists for an example. We recently saw an otherwise excellent book go astray because the author invited the opinions of too many people, including her graphic artist. The artist began to have "cute" ideas about the color of the cover and the hue of the spot color on the inside drawings. Her choices, based on "cute" rather than a knowledge of the retail market, produced a book with a cover that was much more feminine than gender-neutral, as the first few versions of the design had been. The artist also talked the author into incorporating other non-mainstream design ideas, including the way the index was set up. Will these cutesy ideas hurt sales? It's hard to tell. The author will never know how many men did not purchase the book because of its color scheme, or how many bookstores or people in the book trade put it aside as nonprofessional.

False experts may be excellent at what they do. But if they are not book professionals, you are taking a chance that you will not end up with a professional product that will be acceptable to the book trade if they try to take on areas of nonexpertise.

Editing

Editing is probably one of the most important aspects of publishing and probably one of the most sensitive to deal with. Some authors are married to their prose, no matter how much polish it needs. Others believe that their books are "camera-ready" because they have had a friend or family member "edit it."

Few writers admit when they first seek a publisher or packager that they need help with editing or organizing their book. Writers can be very sensitive people. Nobody likes to see the red pencil used, but good editing is essential to any book's credibility and success.

From personal experience, we well know the difference between good, constructive editing that polishes, clarifies, organizes, and improves a writer's work, and bad editing, which is nothing more than shuffling words and rewriting without regard to the author's style or meaning. It is often the result of someone else's ego and desire to impose his or her own style on the work. Bad editing does not check word meanings, spellings, or facts. Nothing is worse for your text than bad editing and nothing is better for your manuscript than good editing.

 Don't shoot the messenger! Someone who tells you that your work needs editing is sort of like your best friend who tells you that your breath is bad. You might not like the message, but the advice could save the day. Skilled editors can make your product shine. We cannot say enough good about the value of the constructive editing process.

Other writers may have been told how wonderful their material was by people who didn't want to hurt their feelings or by people who didn't know the reality of the market. Good editors should give advice and make recommendations to improve your book. But don't hesitate to ask questions, challenge changes, or to tell editors why you feel a paragraph or word is important.

Good editing is more than working on sentence structure while maintaining the author's style. It will also include suggestions for expanding sections, strengthening characters, making cuts, or rewriting for clarification. It will note inconsistencies, or the fact that there is no motive for murder. A good editor will check words with a reputable dictionary to see if they are compound or hyphenated, and will double-check usage and for anachronisms. Good editing will fix incorrect punctuation and, if you have double and triple punctuation marks at the end of sentences, tell you to get rid of them.

Tips for screening a prospective editor

Anyone can claim to be an editor. A degree in English is no guarantee of quality, nor is technical proficiency in grammar and spelling an indicator of skill in the finer points of usage or in developmental editing to meet market needs. So who is qualified to edit? And who is qualified to edit the editor? The following methods help you do so.

Always check references, but primarily to learn about work habits, such as ability to follow directions, history of delivering when agreed to, ease of communication, evidence of conscientiousness, and faithfulness to the author's purpose and "voice."

References are less useful for evaluating technical ability. Authors are usually delighted with anyone who finds the obvious gaffes that save them embarrassment or that improve what may have been in sad shape to begin with—even though the result leaves considerable room for more editing.

If you examine samples of work, know that a published version cannot indicate how well the editor's suggestions were implemented or how many later rounds of editing occurred. So try to review the editor's original notations and compare "before and after."

The most reliable method for evaluating several candidates is to interview them and ask for a sample edit of the same three or four pages of text. Compare the results, using at least these five criteria: thoroughness (how extensive and specific are their notations?), clarity (can you understand the suggestions?), attitude (do the queries show respect for the author?), flexibility (are you offered more than one way to approach a problem?), and scope (do the notations suggest that the editor has a broad view of the book, including its audience, market, topic, and purpose?).

In interviewing several editors, be frank about your book's needs and special challenges. But don't do all the talking. Listen for the questions each editor should ask before agreeing to an assignment. Editors reveal their experience, thoroughness, and understanding by asking about the intended audience, writing style, format, production methods and scheduling, marketing plans, quality of editing desired, and much more.

As for comparing fees, don't be misled by low hourly rates, because there's no way to tell how many hours of editing your book will need. A low estimate could mean a superficial job. You usually get what you pay for. If you ask an editor's references what they paid, also ask how many pages were involved, how technical the contents were, and what special challenges the editor faced.

Chris Roerden, M.A., is a freelance book editor with more than thirty-five years' experience in niche publishing.

A book packager or editor should be addressing very basic marketing questions. Who is your reader? If the reader is "the average person," then you should not be writing in the language of an academician or physician. Your vocabulary, examples, and explanations must be geared to your specific audience. A good editor should point you in the right direction. How much time does your reader have to spend on your book? If the intended audience is very busy, you should shorten sections to keep material focused and sparkling to hold interest. Sometimes an editor may suggest reorganizing the entire book, moving the first chapter to a prologue, developing a character, or eliminating an entire section. Be willing to listen to and consider all ideas that will help sell and market your book.

There are many beautifully illustrated picture books for young children with accompanying text that are suitable for a much older age group. The two don't belong together and will kill sales. The illustrations, format, and text must all be appropriate to your end market—the reader. Be prepared to listen and take criticism.

There are also a number of freelance "book doctors" who advertise their availability to authors in need of manuscript surgery. If you are thinking of contracting for editing services prior to dealing with a book packager, be a careful consumer. Through the years we have received many manuscripts that were supposed to have been "edited" by so-called professionals or by friends of the author. Most needed to be redone because the work did not adhere to book style or even acceptable grammar. There were still gaps in the flow and obvious changes in writing style where the editors had inserted material. We have seen what happens when some "professional" editors have entered their own mistakes when they assist with editing or proofreading because they guess at hyphenation, capitalization, and punctuation. Everyone working on your book needs to be using identical editions of the same professional reference books.

Check references and costs. Ask for before and after samples of editors' work. If possible, negotiate fixed prices rather than an hourly rate. If you are dealing separately with editors and book doctors on an hourly basis, and are not careful, the often unexpected cost of editing could end up being more than all other aspects of production. Nonprofessional editors can be helpful in the early stages of developing your book, but are generally a false economy if you depend on them for professional advice.

One of the benefits of being a self-publisher and working with a book packager is that, because you are paying for the production of the book, you are the boss and, as such, you have the right to reject advice if you feel the book doesn't benefit from the editor's suggested changes. Even so, we strongly suggest that you keep an open mind.

> The more you do to provide "clean copy" to the editor, the easier it will be for your book packager or publisher, and the easier it will be on your wallet. By clean copy we mean having spelling, grammar, and punctuation as correct as possible and with no messy handwritten changes in the margins or between the lines.

Competent editors will be looking at the editing job not just sentence by sentence, but to see how your material can be made into a book that has logical continuity and is consistent in its information.

Sometimes your editor will send you back to the keyboard to reorganize or rework a chapter or section; sometimes to the dictionary, a stylebook, the library, or even back to sources to check facts or to provide additional documentation. Or, editors may challenge what you have stated as a fact. A word of advice, don't guess at "facts" even if you are writing fiction. If your story is about a ship sinking in Puget Sound near Tacoma, don't toss a guessed-at depth into the text. Get the exact figure from harbor charts.

You also can save time and cost by cleaning up your manuscript prior to it reaching an editor's pen. A common and easily fixed punctuation error often made by self-publishers is to place the period outside quotation marks in dialogue.

Wrong: She said, "I like cats better".
Right: He said, "The puppy is cuter."

Editors will fix these errors, but you will pay them to do it.

Authors of children's books should *always* have their books edited. Check grammar and punctuation. You don't want children to learn incorrect punctuation from you, or for your book to be rejected by bookstores, reviewers and libraries because your grammar is improper.

We've included some excellent grammar books in our resource list—books that are fun as they refresh us on often confusing spellings and usage (lie, lay; who, whom; eager, anxious).

Book "style"

A good book packager will require that its editors and proofreaders check for "style." What is style? Simply stated, style standardizes spellings, abbreviations, and hyphenation. Style dictates when to use numerals for numbers or when to spell them out, when to italicize

Many authors, to "show respect" for church or government hierarchy, insist on capitalizing all religious and political titles in their text: Bishop, Priest, Pope, President, Congressman, etc. Wrong! Both stylebooks are specific on this issue. A *title* appears before a person's name and should be capitalized: Bishop Scotto, Pope Paul, President Bush, Queen Elizabeth. If the person's title follows the name, it is simply the job name and should be lowercase. Paul Jones, bishop, George W. Bush, president. When used alone, these titles are not capitalized either. For instance, "The priest is coming to dinner with the president and the queen."

Develop a style sheet for your book based on:

Merriam-Webster's Collegiate Dictionary (latest edition)

The Chicago Manual of Style

List specific words that will be capitalized

List how you will do numbers (spell out through ninety-nine), but decide, following stylebook, how you will handle larger numbers.

Make list of compound words as you look them up: tree house, laptop, backyard, and be consistent throughout the book.

When more than one standard is acceptable for spelling, punctuation, hyphenation, or abbreviation, pick your style and stick with it. Some publishers prefer serial commas—one that precedes a conjunction in a series of three or more items: Red, white, and blue. Open punctuation would eliminate the second comma in the series so it would read: Red, white and blue. Sometimes the serial comma is essential for clarity.

titles and when to put them in quotation marks, and when to capitalize words. Use standard stylebooks, such as *The Chicago Manual of Style*, published by the University of Chicago Press, in conjunction with *The Associated Press Stylebook,* and a quality dictionary, such as the latest edition of Merriam-Webster's *Collegiate Dictionary*. Stylebooks provide the book industry with standards. Your use of one will lend professionalism to your text. Sometimes the suggested style changes may differ from your habit, but if you want to be mainstream, then consistency and conformity to book style is important.

For example, teachers have long taught that all literary titles should be underlined or set within quotation marks. But titles are not underlined in book style. They are either placed in italics (books) or within quotation marks (articles). Titles of poems, songs, television shows, movies, newspapers, magazines, and dramatic works have their own rules. Check *The Chicago Manual of Style* for proper style basics.

Typing teachers have taught that you should put two spaces between sentences. Not so for printed material such as books.

Check all compound words, all names, all foreign words, and all abbreviations with the stylebooks and dictionaries.

Only one space should be used, and for good reason. Spaces take up, well, space, and may increase the length, possibly adding to the production cost.

A New England publisher commissioned a freelance writer to write a travel guide about our part of Florida. After the book's publication, the review we read indicated that the writer had either not done enough homework, or perhaps thought nobody would know that some of the restaurants and stores selected for inclusion in the guide had been out of business for more than two years. While it is often said that a bad review is better than no review, we doubt that people will want to purchase a *new* travel guide that has outdated and inaccurate information. The easy way to solve that problem is to double-check facts, including appendix information, just before going to press.

One novelist we know featured a professional assassin as his main character. The assassin's weapons of choice were poison darts and lethal wrestling holds. Editor Chester Baum asked for proof that the type of poison described in the book would function as the author had indicated. Once he and the author had resolved that detail (the author *did* know his poisons), the editor questioned how a particular wrestling hold had proved fatal. As it turned out, Baum had wrestled during his school years. So the author, also a wrestler, and the editor walked together through the book's scene and ended up in the described lock.

"Aha!" said the delighted Baum. He then understood exactly what the author was attempting to describe and was able to recast the sentences so the action was clear.

Not all editorial sessions are that dramatic. But good editing should question, suggest, and improve.

Horror stories about bad editing abound. "Clara," an elderly, legally blind author, dictated her life story to a retired teacher who said she could also edit the material. Clara planned a small press run and presented her book packager with what she insisted was fully edited copy. What Clara could not see was that her "editor" had only guessed at the spellings of cities and countries around the world where Clara had lived. The editor had not verified spellings of foreign terms. She didn't know book style, so that abbreviations and use of numbers/numerals were not proper, and her use of grammar and punctuation would not have made a passing grade in junior high. The packager did not have the heart to tell Clara that she had been scammed and instead took on the responsibility for fixing all the errors—a greater task than had been anticipated in the bid. Clara may not have been able to read the finished book, but her friends and family would. She deserved a decent product and got it.

There may be times that you will want to establish your own style sheet for a book. First, know the rule, or alternatives. In the rare instance when there is no reference in the stylebooks or dictionary that seems appropriate, you and your editors may create your own style. But, remember, be consistent throughout your book and stay as mainstream as possible.

Checking facts

Careful editors will often challenge statements that are presented as facts or assumptions. They will ask you to verify the spelling of names (never guess). Or, they may ask you to recheck dates, such as when an actual event happened, or how something is done. Creative phonetics don't count. Editors should check on names you may drop into your story and will catch that Oliver Wendell Holmes is not that famous painter of seascapes that you alluded to, when you really meant Winslow Homer.

It doesn't matter if you are writing nonfiction, science fiction, short stories, a novel, or poetry. Your details, facts, time, or geographic references, must be accurate or you will lose credibility. If you are writing about a religious group, such as Seventh-day Adventists, don't have them eating red meat—most are practicing vegetarians. And don't send your characters to Disneyland before it was built.

If you are writing about the Revolutionary War, use terminology that was in common use during the period. For example, don't have the ship's captain saying, "I was mesmerized by her beauty." Mesmer had yet to become known for his work with hypnotism at that time, and according to our dictionary "mesmerize" was not used until 1829. Or, don't have a Civil War era teen character say, "Wow. That's cool." In short, don't make things up thinking no one will notice—somebody will, and your credibility will suffer.

Getting permissions and giving credit

If your book draws on the writing of other people, or uses artwork or photographs produced by others, *you will need their permission*—in advance of printing the book. This includes your publishing historic, previously unpublished letters, such as Civil War correspondence.

Obtaining permissions may not be easy, but as a courtesy, for integrity and to protect yourself from a possible lawsuit, it is a must. You will want to have the permissions in hand before you get too far along in the publishing process because if someone denies you the use of a photograph or does not want material quoted, you will have to make changes.

Good packagers and editors will insist that you give appropriate credit within the text, or on your copyright page, and next to photographs. We have heard many horror stories from the Big

 Get permissions in writing. Pay the necessary fees, if any. Err on the side of caution and respect the work of others.

 If you are relying heavily on the material of others, you may want to check with a copyright attorney for the best current legal advice.

Guys and even from small presses about copyright violations and ensuing problems involving both printed material and artwork. Most photography services and book manufacturers will not make negatives of any previously printed photographs without having written permission from the original studio or photographer in their files.

Remember, *giving credit* is not the same as *asking permission*. If you are using someone else's work, you need to ask for permission—in writing—don't plagiarize! (See p. 208 for Web link to examples.) You may want to send your request for permission by certified mail, return receipt requested. That way if your efforts to reach the originator of the work are unsuccessful, your attempts are documented.

If you are commissioning someone to do artwork or your cover design, make sure the artist agrees in writing, *before the job is started,* to do the work "for hire." That's to protect you later on from having the artist claim a share of the profits of your book even though you have paid up front for the art. Sometimes the artist will insist on a limited agreement, which needs to be renegotiated if you plan to use the design on T-shirts or posters for sale rather than for promotional material for the book. You need to understand and include agreements for the new issues of electronic rights. Your agreement needs to address using the copyrighted material you have permission to use as part of a Web site or in some other electronic form, such as an electronic book.

The Chicago Manual of Style includes a valuable section on copyrights and permissions. We have included other excellent references on copyrights—books and Web sites—in our resource list in the appendices. Review them and, if you still are not sure, contact an attorney who specializes in intellectual properties law.

"The blues"

Do all your proofreading and editing *before* you generate your final computer files or camera-ready copy for the printer. Do *not* plan on doing further proofing from the galley proofs or "bluelines."

The bluelines are a mock-up of your book, composed of the pages and cover, and are made either by placing the negatives from which the printing plates will be made over sheets of blueprint paper, then exposing them to light and developing the prints, or increasingly by a digital output process. The sheets are then folded into signatures, trimmed, stapled and arranged as your book will appear. Or, with print-on-demand, a single copy of the book is printed for you to check instead of bluelines.

The inspection of the blues is the last chance for you or your packager have to make sure that everything is placed properly, that the pages are in order, and that the photographs or illustrations are not upside down, flipped, or placed over the wrong caption. If you spot a serious typographic error you can correct it, but remember changes can be very costly at this stage. If the changes are because of errors *you* have made, such as typos, you will be charged for the corrections.

Usually the blues come by overnight delivery and often must be returned the same day, also by overnight delivery. If you do not process them in a timely fashion you may cause a delay in the printing schedule. If you make major changes at blueline stage, you probably will delay the delivery of your book because it will lose its place on the production line at a book manufacturer and will have to be re-scheduled for printing and binding.

A book manufacturer's sales rep gave us this explanation of how the charges are determined for author alterations at the blueline stage for a job using camera-ready copy: "If just one word in the blueline is changed, the line of type has to be reset and pasted on the page ($2.70), then the page needs to be reshot, and a new negative produced and stripped into the flat ($8.70). The total is $12. With the new electronic technologies, corrected files for problem pages need to be submitted and new film created. The per-page cost is about the same.

Scheduling

Although the issue of schedule is discussed in chapter 7, it is germane to your initial conversations with your book packager. If you are planning to sell through wholesale outlets, such as distributors, you and your team must know, and work with, their schedules.

Distributors' catalogs usually come out in January and July for the spring and winter seasons. Know deadlines for getting your ad copy submitted.

Because the cover is usually featured in the ad for your book, you may need to provide a copy of the cover several months ahead of the book's actual production. Therefore, cover decisions may be the first ones you make with a cover designer or through your packager.

Also, ascertain the purchasing schedule for libraries. According to Lawrence Webster, a former public librarian now serving in public relations for the Florida Library Association, most library systems make their greatest expenditures at the start of the fiscal year. Government fiscal years usually start July 1 or October 1. Most corporate and private fiscal years begin January 1 and end December 31.

Once the copies are off the press, it could take three months to have your book established with the distribution network so that it is orderable by bookstores, libraries and the general public. The publication date is the date when the book is widely available to the public, not the date that the book comes off the press.

3 Do your marketing homework

*For people who have never written a book, writing a book seems like the hard part. Those who have written a book discover that that's wrong. **Selling** a book, that's the hard part. And when you sell a book, you discover the real truth: **Marketing** the book, now that's the **really** hard part.*
—Michael Dobson, lecturer, and author of *Managing Up!*, *Coping with Supervisory Nightmares, Exploring Personality Styles* and *Practical Project Management*

Surprised that the chapter on marketing comes near the beginning of this book? Authors, especially those who hope for sales through traditional outlets, such as bookstores and distributors, should let their marketing plans guide their entire project from inception to publication. While we will discuss some of the topics, such as covers, in other sections, we believe that understanding your customer and your market is of primary importance and should guide many of your decisions about the book, from its title to its inside and exterior design. Marketing—reaching the consumer—should drive most decisions.

A simple definition of marketing is this: Find out what the public wants, then meet that need with your product. To know what the public wants, you need to know who will buy or read your book. There are some easy ways to find out.

Your marketing should begin before the first word is typed. It is much harder to find a market for your already written book than it is to research, write, and design a book for a specific market that you have targeted in advance.

In our initial conferences with authors and self-publishers, we ask them to describe their expected buyer and their expected reader. This information will help determine the cover concept, the title, and the material to be included or deleted during the editing process. The buyer is often the reader,

 Do some basic research by talking to bookstore managers and librarians about your topic ideas. They know the market. Then, write a profile of your expected buyer. Include age, education level, and other relevant details, such as characteristics of the expected buyer and expected buying habits. For example, will your book be an impulse buy or something a purchaser will seek out because of its topic? The profile will help you design a book product to fit your market.

but not always. The book may be written for preschoolers, but its cover and subject matter must appeal to the grandparent or parent who will purchase it. What can you put on the book's cover that will appeal to the buyer? How about an endorsement by a well-known educator or child psychologist?

Knowing your buyer is as important as knowing who will read your book. Will a woman select it for a female friend? A son for his father? Will someone choose it because it tells how to successfully change careers? Or is it for the middle-aged klutz who wants a simple guide to home repairs? Identifying your reader will help you make decisions about format and content. If your expected reader is a busy parent or time-challenged executive, your material must be designed to be easily digestible, not an academic tome.

Professional freelance writers usually understand marketing. They research topics that are current, then write about them, often tailoring the basic information to several sources or buyers. Developing a reader profile helps focus their material to each situation.

Other authors may write a series of shorter books based on what could be chapters in a larger book for a specific market, such as for computer buffs or gardeners. These writers know their audience and may even have a contract with a publisher to do the series.

Filling a demand

How do you find out what the public wants? Easy—you ask! Start with your library or local booksellers. Ask each of them what types of books they purchase. You will probably find out that at this point they are not investing much in fiction or poetry, especially if it is produced by unknown writers. But, for several years they have been telling us that they *are* looking for how-to-do-it books, self-help books that are constructive (not whiny or vindictive), unusual travel ideas, ethnic books, biographies and histories, and children's literature that represents diversity or multicultural themes. Regional and local topics are popular with booksellers and regional distributors, such as the news services that stock racks at airports or newsstands, even though rack distributors can be difficult to deal with.

 Nancy Jane Tetzlaff-Berens, owner of Jungle Larry's Caribbean Gardens and Zoological Park, commissioned a freelance writer to write about the famous Tetzlaff family and the history of the parks in Naples, Florida and Cedar Point, Ohio. After more than three decades in the business, Nancy Jane ("Safari Jane") knew exactly who the primary buyers of the book would be, how much they would be willing to pay, and what information and pictures would interest the buyer and reader. That keen marketing knowledge, drawn from extensive knowledge of her customers, prompted the addition of twice as many photographs as originally planned for the book. The photograph that was selected for the cover and the book's retail price were also based on her detailed buyer profile. The book has national appeal because of the number of visitors to the park's two locations for the past thirty years and the family's high profile. In addition, the book, *Living with Big Cats: The Story of Jungle Larry, Safari Jane, and David Tetzlaff,* has an ideal, steady market through the park's gift shop when the book is promoted by announcers at the animal shows or by park staff.

And write about what you know. Our home is in Florida and we have been told repeatedly by bookstore owners that they can't find enough well-produced books about Florida for the state or regional sections of their stores. Why do they want them? Tourists and new and prospective residents want to read all they can about our area, either while they are sunbathing or to take home as a souvenir. We do the same thing when we travel—look for informative books about the places we visit.

Regional topics include fiction, poetry, history, humor, cookbooks or guidebooks. They may be about fishing, recreation, or the flora and fauna of a particular area. Or they might focus on a famous resident or even a popular tourist spot. "Local" can mean that the author is local or that the subject matter is of local or regional interest, such as a seafood cookbook, a guide to shells or shorebirds, or a town history. The book's appearance is important and it must be professional.

"Some self-publishers seem to think that the only thing that matters is the content of the book, not its look. But that's not true," a bookstore owner said. She also wants to see how a book and its author can be tied into promotional events in the store.

"If we don't buy a new book outright, we might take a few copies on consignment, to see if there is a market for the book," independent bookstore managers tell us.

"It's good for local authors to pop in once in awhile to remind us about their books and to see if we should reorder," another said.

This is good advice, because many independent stores are not set up for automatic reorder as your book sells.

To put it bluntly, the public creates the demand for books. Writers who fill that demand with a professional product and aggressively market their book will find outlets in the marketplace.

Titles must be right

Your title is an important part of your marketing strategy. Make it work for you. Get feedback on it from professionals. Be open to change based on their suggestions.

Titles can sell the book, or they can be misleading, offensive, or unintentionally humorous. Read *Bizarre Books* by Russell Ash and Brian Lake for classic examples. Many books are purchased because of their titles rather than their content. If you are writing a self-help book about divorce, don't call it *My Life with the Spouse from Hell*. Turn the title into something more positive, something that other people can relate to and won't feel embarrassed to have on their coffee table. You may end up with much of the same content, but you might find better sales results calling your book *Six Tips for Coping with an Abusive Partner,* or *How to Divorce without Upsetting the Children.*

Next to the design of your cover, your title must deliver the punch that says, "Buy me!"

During a segment of "All Things Considered" on National Public Radio,[11] host Robert Siegel interviewed author André Bernard who had published a book about titles. The book, aptly titled, *Now, All We Need is a Title,* tells what some of the great books were originally called. For example, among preliminary titles for *Gone with the Wind* was *Tote the Weary Load,* and Alex Haley's *Roots* was first termed *Before This Anger. Valley of the Dolls* was titled *They Don't Build Statues to Businessmen.* Bernard noted that, fortunately for several authors, including Margaret Mitchell, the publisher, or maybe a friend, intervened for the better before press time.

You will miss sales opportunities if your title is too cute or too vague. Your book may be overlooked by a regional buyer because you have not mentioned the region the book is about in the title or subtitle. Or your title may have meaning to you, but fails completely to tell a buyer what the book is about.

In 1913, George Lincoln Walton, M.D., wrote a book published by Houghton Mifflin Company. He said, "The selection of a title is no trifling matter . . . I really wanted to put in something about 'fretting the gizzard,' a term . . . defined in *Webster's Dictionary* as 'to vex one's self.' " He notes that it is a term from Butler's *Hudibras.* The good doctor, perhaps with tongue in check, says, "It was only outside pressure that prevented my choosing for a title *The Unfret Gizzard, and How to Achieve it.*" Instead, the more appropriate *Calm Yourself* was selected.

> Keep your title short or put the key elements first if you want it to fit into the microfiche entry and computer systems used by distributors and libraries. These systems typically contain room for only thirty characters. An abbreviated version of the title won't make sense to someone perusing the list for titles about a specific topic.

Consider the impact of each word in your title and subtitle. Certain words appeal to specific markets; others may turn them off. For example, *My Life with the Spouse from Hell* could be written by a very sincere and religious person, but the word "hell," while perhaps aptly describing the marital situation, could turn off other folks who would not use the "H" word or might be uncomfortable with the intensity of the implied emotion. If your book is of a very personal nature, you will have to decide if you are writing simply to ventilate and vindicate, or if you really have a message beyond your own situation. This is a good time to get feedback from retail professionals. When you have decided on your market title the book accordingly.

Bookstores and distributors carry many more types of books than have been described above. You will improve your chances of success in the traditional market if you find out *before* you write your book what subjects will sell.

Unfortunately, most writers do not ask, much less answer, the marketing questions before sitting down at the typewriter or computer. Most have begun with an idea for a poem or story. They write it. They may even illustrate it before they seek an outlet for the results of their creativity. Often they are disappointed that nobody is buying what they have labored so long to produce.

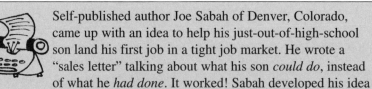 Self-published author Joe Sabah of Denver, Colorado, came up with an idea to help his just-out-of-high-school son land his first job in a tight job market. He wrote a "sales letter" talking about what his son *could do*, instead of what he *had done*. It worked! Sabah developed his idea called the "Gold Form" (after the goldenrod paper on which it was printed) into a book, *How to Get the Job You Really Want and Get Employers to Call You.* Except for a few copies at a local bookstore, Sabah has sold his book exclusively on radio talk shows. Speaking from his home, he talks to audiences all over the country, offering a money-back guarantee on the book. Orders have poured in through his 800 number and he has sold thousands of books.

His marketing system for *How to Get the Job* was so successful that he wrote a second book called *How to Get on Radio Talk Shows All Across America without Leaving Your Home or Office.*

Florida real estate broker Phillip Wilson self-published a book titled *How to Appraise, Buy and Sell a Business.* He sells the book exclusively through seminars he conducts and by word of mouth. The book is set up with occasional workbook-style pages, making its use very personal and therefore not likely to be shared. Wilson is successful in his sales and continues to reprint and update his material regularly. He's found a niche and tied his product in with a guaranteed market, namely his own seminar.

 Rose Sims, a Methodist minister, once was assigned to a small church threatened with closing. However, she turned the church into a thriving, dynamic congregation. She has put her crusade to reopen American's small rural churches into a successful self-published book, *The Dream Lives On.* She conducted church-growth seminars and sold her book at these forums. She has a dramatic story, a good product, and a ready market.

Dealing with the obvious

Sometimes the answers to the basic marketing questions seem obvious. For example, one of the first questions we ask people who come to us having written a children's story or picture book is this: For what age child have you written your book? Surprisingly, most writers aren't sure, even though they have already completed the story—and the illustrations to accompany it.

The age of the reader is critical to the presentation of the material. Books for young children use a lot of color inside and out. But the picture book appearance would not appeal to upper-elementary school students. Older elementary students like "chapter books"—books divided into chapters. Reading a book with chapters is a milestone showing that these preteens want to identify themselves with the adult rather than with the picture book market.

We also ask: How difficult is the vocabulary and does it fit with the age child the book is written for? Are challenging words a plus for parents who may want to enrich their children's language skills? Do the illustrations make sense, and are they well placed? Does the book have a message? Has this book been "done" a million times, such as an alphabet book? If so, yours needs to have a different twist or it won't compete well with the other books already in the stores.

Ask the experts

Beginning (and even professional) writers who are serious about publishing books for children can easily get good marketing feedback on the appropriateness of the material to various age groups, as well as the book's overall salability, by taking two very simple steps.

First make some copies of your manuscript and give it to families with children to read and critique. Children love to give advice. Take their opinions seriously. Did they think the beginning needs to have more action? Could they tell you what the book was about? Did they like the characters and find them interesting? Ask each child reader what age group would best like the book. Kids know.

Next, take your materials to a bookstore and to the library. Look at what the competition will be for your book. Talk to staff members and ask them if your idea has possibilities, then listen to what all these experienced resource people tell you. Their answers will be constructive, and will help guide your publishing decisions.

Other considerations

Traditionally, self-publishers have sold their books through bookstores and to libraries. These outlets are still an important part of today's options but they may be less important than they have been in the past. Most book experts counsel that you should *not* expect your best sales from bookstores. Remember that the Big Guys are sinking huge dollars into national campaigns. There are more than 135,000 new titles published every year, and that's a lot of books from which to pick, and a lot of competition for your title. When you are making your initial decisions about your market, consider these alternatives:

- selling through catalogs
- sales through direct mail to either your own or a commercial mailing list
- sales at seminars (talk about your subject and sell books)
- sales through talk shows
- sales through the Internet

 Take a look at your material. Can you create a package with your book, yourself, and tapes or videos? Does your topic lend itself to promotion on radio talk shows or to direct mail sales? Identify potential audiences to target, and go after them.

Will your topic appeal to a specific segment of the population? Do you know if there are clubs or organizations with a particular interest in your subject? For example, self-publisher Donald Moyer Wilson knew that books about Amelia Earhart have a ready audience. His marketing for *Amelia Earhart: Lost Legend* (Enigma Press) appropriately targeted Earhart researchers, Earhart society members, the media, aviation buffs, and members of Zonta International, of which Earhart was a member. In addition to other media, Don Wilson's book was reviewed in the Earhart Society newsletter, and he sold his book during talks he gave around the country. To stimulate sales, Wilson sent out direct-mail fliers and taught a class about Earhart. Because it was packaged properly, it was available for distribution nationwide, and was in its second printing within six months.

In planning your book, consider how you will let the potential buyers know about it through direct mail, print ads, talk shows, or seminars. Many successful self-publishers have found a market niche and filled it. Some use seminars and talk shows to sell their books, often including the price of their book in the seminar fee. This technique guarantees sales.

 Authors Steve Wood and Jim Burnham wrote *Christian Fatherhood: The Eight Commitments of St. Joseph's Covenant Keepers*, which is sold through small groups for men generally within the Catholic Church. Wood is the founder of an organization called St. Joseph's Covenant Keepers. The idea behind the movement is to help men become better fathers, to accept responsibility for their wives and children, and to find a new life within the church. His book had powerful endorsements: a letter from Mother Teresa, professors, archbishops, authors, and two professional football players and a Navy SEAL. Wood knows that men—his target market— will respond to words from athletes who have excelled, such as Rick Strom, a former NFL quarterback with the Pittsburgh Steelers/Buffalo Bills. The book is sold through St. Joseph's Covenant Keepers' seminars and retreat weekends. Wood is effectively adding collateral material—a workbook and videotape—with the same the same cover, which shows a father and son fishing. Family Life Center Publications has published a second book, *The ABCs of Choosing a Good Husband,* and sell both through its Web site, www.dads.org.

Author Thomas Coughlin has come up with an inventive marketing technique. He has placed framed posters for his racy romance novel, *Maggie May's Diary,* in women's rest rooms in various places in Wells Beach, Maine. Wells Beach is the setting of a significant portion of the book. One such rest room in this popular tourist location is in the Maine Diner, which conveniently has an adjacent gift shop. Coughlin, in his third printing of the book, has sold more than 400 copies in the diner gift shop. Now that's target marketing!

You can market a book by its cover

You many not be able to judge a book by its cover, but you sure can use the cover to sell the book! Part of your preliminary marketing planning will include determining the elements you will use in cover design. While we will be discussing cover design later in more detail, consider this: Your cover is an advertisement for your book. In fact, for those who are not specifically seeking your book, the cover is the single most effective advertisement you have.

> Always order an overprint of your cover so you have enough to give one to each salesperson at each sales organization. Several hundred extra covers is a good number. If you don't you may be asked to submit twenty books to the distributor. The covers will then be removed from them for the salespeople to carry with them on the road. There is no point in wasting good copies of your books.

> Cover! Cover! Cover! You *must* have a professional cover! This sermon is preached by every distributor and book buyer. According to Chris Pearl of Incite Graphic Design, "Look for these credentials: A graphic artist who has a well-rounded background, such as a classical fine arts degree, and at least a decade of successful experience in book cover design."

Richard Capps, former director of product development for Unique Books, Inc., a library distributor for many small and independent publishers, said that new nonfiction books are not necessarily selected for their content (no buyer has time to read them all), but for their covers and titles. Unique's salespeople, like those of other distributors, do not carry thousands of books with them when they call on libraries—they carry book covers. Ron Watson, a book buyer at Ingram Books—

a major wholesale company—says the cover must be able to sell the book within *seven* seconds.

Librarians and buyers for bookstores will also judge your book by the cover and your title—also in just a few seconds.

The colors, choice of typeface, the design elements, and layout can be critical to a sale. Professional cover designers know what makes a dynamic cover, and they know how the combined elements convey a message to make your book look like other books in its category, or like no other book in its genre.

If you consider the cover is a billboard or advertisement for the book, then use it to sell the book. In addition to the artistic elements incorporated in the cover, and the title itself, you may need to include a subtitle to give the reader some additional information about the book's content.

We have seen covers with good art fail the professional "test" because the artist, not the cover designer, dictated where the type should go—so as not to cover his or her artwork. One artist, who did the cover for a lovely poetry book about shorebirds for children, was adamant that the title not obscure any of the picture she had painted. As a result, there was no information about the book's content on the cover. The title was obscure and poetic. There was no subtitle or verbiage noting that this was a regional book for children. The book did not sell well after the initial flurry of publicity. The artist understood art, but not marketing, or what is essential to a book cover.

Endorsements as advertising

Getting experts, influential people, or people with important (and relevant) careers to read and write a comment on your book can be a powerful selling point. Their blurbs, as they are referred to in the trade, placed prominently on the front or back cover, will help lend credibility to your book and

Don't be afraid to write sample blurbs and send them off to the persons you want to sign them. If they are willing to endorse your book, they will write their own sentences, possibly based on your suggestions, or approve what you have provided.

may just be what you need to persuade a potential buyer into making the purchase.

Endorsements can be very important, no matter what the subject of your book. Suppose you have written a nonfiction book about divorce, or child abuse, home health care, exercise physiology, or gardening. If you are not recognized as an authority in the field of your subject matter, but know your material is accurate and comprehensive, get people with credentials or name recognition to read it and lend their support through an endorsement. To meet your deadlines, start gathering endorsements before the book is completed by letting potential endorsers read an early draft or chapter outline. Write a suggested blurb for them to use.

Even if you, the author, are well known, endorsements will help make sales. If you are an entertainer who has written an autobiography, don't hesitate to call on fellow showbiz colleagues to be quoted as saying something like, "Great backstage stories" or "A real page-turner. I couldn't put it down." Or, "Authoritative in the field." Their names and comments will help sell your book.

If your previous material has been favorably reviewed, work that into your back cover, jacket flaps, or front matter. If your book wins a prize, have foil stickers printed stating the award information and affix them to the cover of each copy you send out. If your book has been reviewed, mention the reviewer and positive quotes in your publicity or next edition of the book. If the review was negative, just mention that you were "reviewed by . . ." and skip the quotes. At least the book reached the review stage! Don't be shy about promoting yourself!

The price must be right

The retail price of your book is a very important part of your marketing considerations. Compare the prices of books like yours at the bookstore or on the Internet. If comparable books are selling in the range of $12.95 to $14.95, certainly you would not want to price your book at $25.95. Consumers probably wouldn't buy your book at the much higher price unless you have produced something really special. But don't underprice your book either; it will appear that it doesn't have value. Try to hit the middle range. That is easier if you have properly sized your press run and do not order so few books that you have to price them too high for sales.

Big Guys usually price their products at least seven to nine times the unit production cost, but because they are printing in such large quantities, the unit production cost is quite low. It is very difficult for the small publisher or self-publisher to afford to do a large enough press run to put a reasonable, competitive price on the product and still be able to make a profit when the books are discounted to distributors, wholesalers, or to bookstores (see chapter 7 for a discussion of discount schedules).

We recommend that you try to balance the size of your press run, the size of your wallet, and the "sticker" price of your book—taking into consideration the way you expect to sell it, through wholesalers or at retail. If you do this carefully you should be able to at least break

 Esther Mockler decided to celebrate her ninety-first birthday by writing and publishing the story of raising her family on a ranch in Wyoming during the Great Depression. Her elegantly written *Eighty Miles from a Doctor* goes beyond her personal memoirs. It is a marvelous tale of what ranching was like in the 1930s and 1940s. Her husband was head of the cattlemen's association and was eventually elected to the state House of Representatives where he served as speaker. Esther helped establish libraries and collected oral histories from pioneers, in addition to raising four children and feeding strangers during hard economic times on a remote cattle ranch.

She developed a marketing plan while her book was in production. She received glowing endorsements from then U.S. Senator Alan K. Simpson, and Cliff Hansen, former U.S. senator and Wyoming governor.

Her family obtained a list of bookstores in Wyoming (the population being as small as it is, they knew many of the bookstore owners) and arranged book signings and speaking engagements at stores and homes as soon as the book was off the press. Esther flew from her home in Florida for her author tour in Wyoming, and within two months she had sold more than 1,000 copies. When she returned home she continued her marketing through television, book signings, and speaking engagements.

even on your production costs when you have sold about half of the first printing. Many authors choose to only do a short first run and deliberately price their books at very close to cost in the hope that with good sales, they will be able attract a major publisher or perhaps an agent. If they don't, when they sell out they will have just about broken even anyway.

 Massachusetts poet Nancy Miller has seen how self-publishing can bring success. She began by publishing selected poems in two cooperative anthologies. "First, there was a flurry of press about the anthology, and people beyond my friends and family began to see me as a poet. I was invited to judge a poetry contest for the *Lawrence Eagle-Tribune* and subsequently was asked to be a part of some poetry readings. As a result, a local freelance writer interviewed me for an article in an insert to our weekly regional newspaper. My circle of author acquaintances and friends widened, leading to new knowledge of writing workshops that I was able to attend."

"As my visibility increased, I began to take myself as a poet more seriously. I felt the confidence to submit my work to various publications and contests. After the national magazine *Mediphors* accepted one of my poems, I submitted to other journals and anthologies. Although there were maybe forty rejection slips for each success, I was committed to sharing my work. The anthology *Our Mothers, Our Selves,* published by Bergin & Garvey, printed one of my poems alongside works by Robert Bly, Maya Angelou, Maxine Kumin, and Sharon Olds. Elated and validated, I am even more committed to sharing my voice."

Miller self-published *Dance Me Along the Path*, a volume of her work, and a book of columns about her town—*Of Minitmen & Molly's.* "I prefer to self-publish so that I can retain the control (once one of my poems appeared in a newsletter with the critical last line missing), both artistically and financially. I have seen chapbooks of disappointing quality and I know fine poets who suffer commercial rejection again and again. Walt Whitman's first printing of *Leaves of Grass* was self-published; sometimes editors misjudge good material."

Your marketing costs will also cut into your profit, but in the long run, if you plan carefully, you should be able to recoup your investment or even make a profit.

Your professional advisors or packager should be able to help you price your book.

Small markets

Perhaps your material is of more limited interest, such as a book of poetry, personal philosophy, or maybe even a family history. How you package your book will depend on your pocketbook and your potential audience. If you anticipate selling one hundred copies of a clan history to family members at a reunion, and perhaps a few more to friends or to the local bookstore, you will want to make your packaging or printing decisions on that basis.

Many poets test the market for their work by having a chapbook printed. Chapbooks are typically low-budget productions with one-color covers, but need not look unprofessional if care is taken to have the book set up properly and proofread carefully. The chapbook is not likely to reach a wide commercial market, but will satisfy the author's need to have poems in book form.

If you aren't sure about how extensive the market is for your material, take samples of the pages or a chapter to a bookstore or library. Then listen carefully to what is being said about the market. A small press run will get you into print, with the satisfaction of having a book. If you are realistic about the demand for your product, you won't have 10,000 copies produced and then find out too late that nobody is buying that type of book or that you do not have the marketing resources or stamina to sell it.

According to a poll conducted by *ForeWord* magazine,[12] independent booksellers appreciate having sales representatives call on them about titles, like to see galleys and sample chapters prior to publication, and read direct mail. Eighty-four percent said they purchased books based on trade reviews. Self-published books must be professionally produced and properly credentialed to get the attention of trade reviewers and the independent stores outside your region.

You might also consider testing the market by having some of your work published in a cooperative poetry or literature anthology. In a cooperative anthology, each contributor shares in the cost of the production of the book. When the book is published, participants receive a share of the press run in proportion to the share of the costs they underwrote. Then you practice your salesmanship and gauge the reception of your work with the public.

Cooperative anthologies should be fully credentialed for retail sales. These anthologies are a relatively inexpensive method of having your work published. Not only are these anthologies a good means of getting your work in print, they are an invaluable opportunity for you to develop your marketing abilities and salesmanship.

Niche markets

Silhouettes: Rediscovering the Lost Arts by Katheryn Flocken-Henriquez is a niche book with tremendous sales potential. If you think the book's market is craft and art stores and speciality catalogs, you might be surprised to learn that it, and a companion silhouette kit, are being sold at Walt Disney World. Shortly after it was released, the author contacted Disneyland plus the overseas Disney theme parks for similar sales outlets. She had an excellent review in *American Papercutters,* so orders came in before the book was off the press.

"I think the draw is that the information has been top secret for 250 years, and here's how to do it," she said. The Disney connection makes sense because silhouette artists are on location crafting their art for tourists.

A niche market. An age-old secret revealed, possibly creating controversy and media coverage. A how-to-do-it and kit. Excellent marketing plan and smart strategies and this self-publisher is headed for major success.

Riding the horse

If success strikes through your own efforts or serendipity, will you be ready? Ready to "jump on the horse and ride it until it drops," as Robert James Waller, author of *The Bridges of Madison County* told booksellers at the American Booksellers Association trade show in Miami. He seemed surprised at the success of his novel and the various salable spin-offs, such as calendars. But he planned on capitalizing on the book's commercial success as long as possible. Small presses, such as Health Communications Inc. may not be very well known as a publishing name, but its "Chicken Soup" series continues to have unprecedented national appeal. There is "Chicken Soup" on the shelves for just about every age person and their situations. And the "canning" continues.

Self-publishers, such as J. P. Polidoro, also can find themselves in the national spotlight. In the fall of 2001, Polidoro's Longtail Publishing released his second novel, *Project Samuel: The Quest for the Centennial Nobel Prize.* Polidoro had combined his interest in baseball and baseball memorabilia and his background in reproductive biology to write about the cloning of baseball great Ted Williams. Polidoro hoped that the book would sell because it was the year of the Nobel centennial, and his characters were headed to Stockholm for the ceremony. What he hadn't anticipated was that on July 5, 2002, Ted Williams himself would die and an incredible family feud would start over what to do with his remains. Two of Williams's children wanted to have the body cryogenically frozen in the hope that he could be restored to life at some future point. Another family member objected.

And there was Polidoro, thrust into prime time. His book almost immediately became the subject of newspaper articles around the nation. A chapter of the book was reproduced on ESPN's Web site. Polidoro was invited on talk shows, including New England Cable News and CNN Headline News. During the latter, the book's cover was shown a number of times and the interviewer said the book was available on Amazon.com. In the two weeks since the media interest in *Project Samuel* began, the book had climbed from a ranking of 325,000 on Amazon.com's site, to 45,000 to 4,000 after the CNN mention, and his first book, *Rapid Descent*, also showed increased sales. He didn't wait for additional interviews. He was busy contacting major networks to make himself available at any hour of the night or day.

Marketing checklist

Professional book publicists and agents know that marketing must begin *before* the book is published. Among the elements for you to consider while developing a marketing plan:[13]

- Look: Title, pricing, jacket or cover concept, overall format and page design
- Positioning: Who is the buyer? The reader? The distributor? The bookseller? The reviewer?
- Publicity: The "must" review; media; targeted media, press release as book review, local area publicity opportunities, and never forget word-of-mouth, the best publicity of all.
- Sales: Specialty retailers or wholesalers not covered by your distributor, order forms, representation at national and regional trade shows and other conventions
- Subsidiary rights: Serial, syndication, book clubs, foreign rights, paperback, electronic

Early on, before your book is released, a consultation with an experienced book-marketing firm could be a tremendous benefit for exposure and sales. Before hiring a firm, ask for references and talk to a number of their clients, past and present.

4 Creating a professional product

If we want the same treatment that the big publishers get, we need to act like professional publishers. Instead of bucking the system, we must learn to fit into the professional publishing community.
—Christopher Carroll, publisher

You've probably heard the old expression "penny-wise and pound-foolish." We want you to know that applied to producing a book, the value of this age-old caution is more than sound. You can have a brilliant idea and a terrific story, but if you skimp on the necessary costs of book production, or ignore the traditional setup of a book, you may well doom your entire product to failure.

Producing a book is similar to selling a house. The house may be structurally sound, but if it lacks "curb appeal," because the outside is a mess, or if the inside is poorly designed, it won't fare well against the competition.

Books, like all products, must meet certain standards to compete in the marketplace. There are, unfortunately, many self-published books that by their very look proclaim that they are homemade.

Don't get us wrong. There are times when the homemade look may not matter much—when, for instance, a self-publisher with a small budget anticipates a limited readership. People will purchase the book because they know the author, because there is a local angle, or because the book is produced by a local writers' club for its members.

A construction paper or cardstock cover, printed in one color and handbound over a book that has been photocopied from typewritten copy, might be all right for some book projects, but remember, aside from a possible courtesy placement by a local independent bookstore, it won't be widely salable.

Some authors think they can be successful by simply taking copy they have generated on their computer or typewriter directly to the printer, instead of having their work professionally prepared. They may have done the cover design themselves or perhaps had a friend draw the art. In the end, they have a book in hand, but because they have taken the least expensive route and have declined professional guidance, their book looks amateurish inside and out. Lack of salability should not come as a surprise.

We believe it is just as easy, and not much, or perhaps, any more expensive, to make a book look good, as it is to allow it to be done with an unprofessional appearance. Working with reputable professionals or book packaging service should ensure that you will deal with all the significant components necessary to produce a quality book.

Gene Starner, a regional buyer for Barnes & Noble, underscores the need for books to be professionally produced, fully credentialed, properly priced, and available through a wholesaler in order to be carried by in-mall bookstores or the superstores, such as Barnes & Noble, Borders/Walden, or Books-A-Million. Only if a book meets the standards, both inside and out, can it be considered for its subject matter.

What are credentials?

The first thing your book needs are the proper credentials. Credentials are the "fingerprints" of your book, making it identifiable and salable. If you have any plans to market your book to stores, libraries, catalogs, or distributors, you must have it credentialed. Without credentials, you will have as much luck as if you were trying to show a mutt at the Westminster Kennel Club.

The most important credential is your International Standard Book Number or ISBN. The ISBN system is voluntary, but has been adopted internationally by virtually all publishers, distributors, and bookstores. Your ISBN is a unique, ten-digit number that identifies you as publisher and your book. An ISBN is never recycled; it is permanently assigned to a specific version of a book. Each version of your book (hardcover, softcover, disk, or tape) will need to have its own ISBN.

ISBNs are issued to publishers by the R. R. Bowker Company in groups of ten, one hundred, or more, depending on the expected number of publications per year. The ISBNs are then assigned in ascending numerical order by the publisher from the list to their books.

By agreement between Bowker and publishers, the ISBN must be printed on the verso, or copyright page and on the lower right-hand corner of the outside back cover, usually above the EAN Bookland bar code.

Copyright © 1995 Tabby House

All rights reserved; no part of this publication may be reproduced, stored in a retrieval system, or transmitted, in any form or by any means, electronic, mechanical, photocopying, recording, or otherwise, without the prior written permission of Tabby House.

Manufactured in the United States of America
Library of Congress Catalog Card Number: 95–35376
ISBN: 1–881539–03–2
Illustrations: Christopher Grotke
Page design: Abigail Grotke
Cover design: Pearl & Associates
Setup and typography: Bob Lefebvre

Library of Congress Cataloging-in-Publication Data
Salisbury, Linda G. (Linda Grotke)
    Smart self-publishing : an author's guide to producing a
marketable book / Linda and Jim Salisbury : with foreword by Joe Sabah.
          p.   cm.
    "Hot tips, sound advice, and publishing adventures from authors,
distributors, librarians, and book buyers."
    Includes index.
    ISBN 1–881539–03–2
    1. Self-publishing --United States.   I. Salisbury, Jim, 1936–
II. Title.
Z289.5.S25   1995
070.5'93--dc20   95–35376

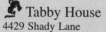 Tabby House
4429 Shady Lane
Charlotte Harbor, Florida, 33980
(941) 629-7646

The verso page from our first edition shows information that must be included.

This edition of *Smart Self-Publishing* is assigned 1-881539-30-X as its ISBN. The first digit represents the country of origin, the United States. The second group of six digits is the publisher prefix, identifying Tabby House as the publisher. The third pair, 30, tells which book this is in the sequence of books Tabby House has published using this particular "bank" or group of ISBNs. The final character is a "check," which mathematically proves that the rest of the number is valid.

Bowker also publishes *Forthcoming Books in Print* and *Books in Print*—comprehensive listings that provide pertinent information about books to book buyers.

Credentials are important if customers want to order a book through a bookstore. The ISBN will let the store track a book back to a publisher. Without the ISBN, sales to stores, including those on large Internet stores, are easily lost.

Bar code

Like the ISBN, the EAN Bookland bar code contains important information that is useful to stores for point of sale information. When the bar code is scanned or entered into the computerized cash register, in addition to the price and tax coming up on the register, the appropriate inventory control information is entered into the system. In some cases, the systems are part of the store's distribution inventory system, and will automatically reorder from the wholesaler or distributor.

The bar code is a series of vertical bars encoded with the title, and ISBN. The price of your book is indicated by another, smaller bar code next to the EAN bar code. Bar codes are usually produced as a negative and are provided to the cover designer on film or disk to be incorporated directly into the composite film for the convenience of the printer. The bar code typically is printed on the back cover of a softcover book and on the jacket of a hardcover edition.

It's easy to get a bar code produced. There are many bar code services (see appendix D) that make them up for about twenty-five dollars, and can get them to you very quickly. Many book manufacturers and cover designers also have the equipment to produce bar codes at a low cost. The bar code is an essential part of the credentials package. In fact, distributors, wholesalers and larger bookstores will refuse books that do not have one. The bar code increases the book's professional appearance and, more importantly, will enhance retail salability.

Make sure the bar code is printed on the back cover of your book. A self-publisher we know had a beautiful nature scene on his four-color cover. He didn't want to mess up the design with the bar code or other standard back cover information, and so he had the bar code printed inside the jacket. Bad move. Buyers at chain bookstores raved about his production, but said they couldn't carry it without the bar code on the back cover.

Make sure the bar code and ISBN are correct before the book goes to press. Sometimes the person creating the bar code for you may make an error. Find it by checking the ISBN and price before the cover is printed.

Artwork should never dictate what goes on the cover, or the placement of the lettering. Don't leave off important information out of deference to an artist who says, "Don't cover up my art with your title."

Copyright, Library of Congress Control Number, and PCIP

The rest of your credentials are located on the copyright or verso page. All left-hand pages are verso pages, but *the* verso page is the one on the back of the title page. You should also put the book's credentials on the back cover. Right-hand pages are called "recto" pages.

Under 1984 copyright laws, your work is copyrighted to you as soon as you put the words on paper. You don't need to have your book officially registered with the copyright office prior

We have seen self-published books in which authors actually print on the verso page, "Library of Congress Number pending" or some such silly thing. Perhaps the authors didn't understand how to get the credentials they need, or why they are important.

to publication. In fact, if you do, it will make things a bit more complicated, as you will have to explain why you are trying to copyright the same material twice. If you are concerned about your copyright, put the copyright symbol ©, the year, and your name on the bottom of each manuscript page when you send your unfinished book to publishers, magazines, or editors.

The copyright notice should be printed on the verso page of your book. Once the book is off the press, you or your packager should fill out the copyright application (Form TX) and send it, along with the fee (thirty dollars at this printing), and two copies of the book to the Register of Copyrights at the Library of Congress.

> If your book is going to be delivered from the book manufacturer late in the year, but the date of publication (when it will be available to the public at the bookstores) won't be until after January 1, you should put the new year's copyright date on it so you can have a "new book" for as long as possible.

If you are selling the rights to your book or working with a subsidy publisher, e-publisher, or vanity press, be sure to resolve the issue of who will hold the copyright *before* you sign the contract. Once your book is published, it may be too late. Although you paid for the cost of the entire production, you may no longer own the all the rights.

For marketing purposes, the year of publication should coincide with the year of copyright. Distributors and buyers unfortunately make the assumption that if the copyright year is not the current year, that the material is old and should be on the "backlist." The backlist refers to releases from previous years that are still available from a distributor, but are not as actively promoted. You can update the copyright if you make significant changes in your book for a later edition.

The Library of Congress offers two services to authors, which must be initiated *before* your book is published. The one used by most self-publishing authors and many small presses is called the Preassigned Control Number (PCN) program. The Library of Congress has recently decided to dispense with paper applications for control numbers. All applications are now being submitted via the Internet. You must first go to the Electronic Preassigned Control Number (EPCN) home page (http://pcn.loc.gov/pcn) and register as a publisher. Once you are accepted in the program you will be given a user name and password so you can log in and apply for a preassigned control number for your book. You will need your ISBN before you register.

It usually takes a few days for your initial application to be acted on and accepted, then it will take a week or so for your control number to be assigned, so don't wait until the last minute to apply. You will need to have this number printed in your book on the verso page for catalog cards in libraries. Obviously, you cannot get a *pre*assigned number *after* the book is printed.

The second, called the Cataloging in Publication (CIP) Program, is used for books that are expected to be widely used in libraries. Publishers who wish to take advantage of this service must make application to the Library of Congress and be registered as members of the program.

There is a lengthy application to be filled out, and either all or a significant portion of the final draft of the book must be submitted for review. If you, as a publisher, are registered with the CIP program and the book fits the criteria, you will receive CIP data to print on the verso page, *exactly as provided.* CIP data is sent to libraries on microfiche and is duplicated on library cards for catalogs, making the librarian's job easier.

Self-publishers and one-book publishers are not accepted by the Library of Congress for the CIP program, but some book manufacturers and some library distributors will create PCIP (Publisher's Cataloging in Publication) for a small fee. This is a big help if you do not qualify for the governmental program. Use their services if you want PCIP cataloging information to print on the verso page. The PCIP makes your book more attractive to the library market.

Remember, after your book is finished and you have copies in hand, you or your packager will need to send one copy to the Library of Congress and two copies, with the appropriate fee and completed application, to the copyright office.

About your book's cover

What is the first thing you notice about a book? For most people it is the cover, front, back, and spine. It's surprising, though, how many do-it-yourself self-publishers have only the front cover printed. The spine and back cover are left blank, an immediate sign of an unprofessional product. Some e-book publishers even use *your* back cover as an advertisement for *their* own services. This will not help your sales.

Richard Capps, formerly of Unique Books, a library distribution service, told us what companies like Unique consider in the selection of new titles to present to librarians across the country: "I look at the cover, the quality of the binding and to see if the book has a table of contents, index, and cataloging in publication. I'll open it up and pull on the book rather aggressively to determine if its binding will withstand the library circulation."

We have heard that a library distributor actually may fling a book across the room to see how well it holds together. Library books must be able to withstand hard use and misuse.

Capps noted that librarians, faced with making selections from as many as 2,300 titles in the salesperson's catalog, and looking at many covers in only two or three hours, may not have time to read the data slip accompanying the book's cover.

What does sell the book? "Covers, covers, covers and titles. Does the book look professionally done? The cover is what catches your eye, and it is what catches the librarian's eye," said Capps.

Cover design

Book cover design is itself a specialty field, and within it cover designers are often known for individual specialties. Some may be very good at science fiction covers, or medical/textbook covers, children's books, or romance novels, for example.

You will need to have an eye-catching cover that is mainstream for your type of book, and that usually means giving up your own design ideas and Cousin Ella's art. Or, at the very least, let a professional cover designer work with your ideas.

Book packagers should have a number of professional designers either on staff or available as freelancers. Or get names of professional designers from publishers' associations. Professional cover artists will be able to create a well-designed cover to fit virtually every budget and every book. If you are hiring a professional cover designer to do the cover of your book, you can expect to pay from $1,500 upwards for the work.

You or your packager will also give direction to the artist by discussing the overall concept of the book and its title, and perhaps suggest some elements to be used, such as photographs. Many designers like to have several chapters to read to help stimulate subject-oriented ideas. The cover designer should submit two or three sketches or concepts for your consideration. You should have an opportunity to see these and choose between, or combine elements from the options. Don't make your packager and artist try to read your mind. If you have a vision of what your cover should look like, share it.

We suggest that you first go to some bookstores to see what type covers new books (with the current year's copyright) in your genre are featuring. You want your book to be striking, but it also needs to fit in with the other books on the shelf. Then, listen to the professionals you have hired. Had we dictated to our cover designers what we thought this book's cover, or the cover used on the first two editions, should be like, we never would have ended up with this design, which we think is the right concept.

Authors can run up production costs and lose time if they fail to communicate their ideas until after preliminary designs are completed,

Don't try to micromanage the design of your cover. Don't show it to every nonexpert you know for input. Each will tell you something different about the cover's color, or the type of font, or the wording of the subtitle. If you must get a second opinion, ask the manager at the bookstore. A project that should take four months, may end up taking a year, and end up looking like it was put together by a committee of amateurs rather than an expert, even if you have hired professionals. And the cost will increase every time you decide to tinker with something at the suggestion of yet another "consultant."

then trying to dictate every aspect of the project. If you have hired professionals, let them do their job.

We know of an author who so micromanaged the cover design that, even though a professional designer was involved, the cover was not professional. Not surprisingly, a committee evaluating books for inclusion in chain stores told the author that while they liked his book and would recommend its placement, the cover (5,000 already printed but not bound) was unacceptable. The author begged the now very frustrated designer to do just one more version. The designer said he would—but only if the author would let him do his job without interference. The author agreed and the result was a stronger, more colorful, professional rendition. However, the author couldn't stay out of it, and immediately wanted fonts and colors changed again. His cover costs kept increasing, time was wasted, and with a micromanaged, weakened cover, there was no guarantee that it would be any more acceptable than the one rejected by the bookstore committee.

Unless you are a professional cover designer, the chances are that you should trust the professional's layout, colors, and design. Book-cover designers should know what works in the marketplace and what constitutes a good cover for your book.

Since you are paying for their expertise, listen to the experts. But, if you really dislike a particular color, be sure to let it be known so the artist does not inadvertently come up with a color scheme that will make you say, "Yeech!" Keep in mind, though, what you consider to be "yeech!" may well be a customer-friendly color that will help sell the book.

> Librarians recommend that when you design your spine, leave room at the bottom for librarians to stick on cataloging information without covering the title or author's name.

> Don't use the word "by" in association with your name as the author, unless it is an "edited by" or you have prior works in print so that you are indicating that the new title is "by the author of. . . ." Use of "by" is a sign of an amateur production.

Your book's back cover is a full-page advertisement, and it is important that you make full use of it. There are certain elements you need to include: the retail price, the bar code, the ISBN, and the imprint of the publisher (name and/or logo). In addition, you should supply your packager or cover designer with endorsements, a concise and compelling description of the content, and, if you think it will help sales, a photo of yourself and your biographical information.

And don't laugh at this reminder: Be sure to include your name on the cover. We *have* seen books printed without the author's name on the cover! But unless you are very well-known, don't make your name the focal point—good design or the title will sell the book even if your name is unfamiliar.

The spine is an essential part of any book's professional look and its marketability. It needs to have the book's title and the author's name on it, the publisher's imprint, and maybe the ISBN. It should also make a dramatic visual statement, so when the book is shelved spine out, as nine out of ten books are, it will have a better chance to catch the attention of browsers. Spines should be colorful or eye-catching. Make sure you have a professional spine.

To sum up, there are hundreds, if not thousands, of books in the typical bookstore, and if your book is to sell, it must be competitive. The average buyer, unless on a specific mission to buy a particular book, must be drawn to your cover. If bookstore browsers pick up your book it is because the front cover, the spine, or the title has caught their eye. After looking at the front cover, they usually flip the book over and look at the back cover and read the blurbs. Your book needs to be screaming, "Read me!" If the title and covers have done their job, potential buyers will probably look at the dust jacket flaps or leaf through the book for additional information. Most decisions are made in just a few seconds. Check out your own book-buying habits. Ask your friends what factors make them decide to buy an "unknown" book.

Between the covers

If you are like most people, you have been reading books all your life without giving much more than cursory thought to book format. A half-title page. What's that?

For your self-published book to compete in the marketplace of bookstores and libraries, you must include in it all the relevant, traditional elements of books. It is important that you hire experts, either on your own or through your book packager, to do those things that are outside of your expertise, such as formatting, cover and page design, typesetting, and indexing.

For a detailed explanation of the anatomy of a book, we recommend reading *The Chicago Manual of Style*. Meanwhile, here are some of the basics that you should know. Between the covers of most books there are three distinct sections: the front matter, the body of the book, and the back matter. Depending on the book's purpose, the content of each of those sections will vary. A novel is not likely to need an index, but may have a lengthy introduction or a list of characters. A science fiction or fantasy may need a glossary of invented terms, plus a listing of characters and maps.

The front matter has page numbers printed in italic Roman numerals (except for any blank or "white" pages, which do not have any numbers or headers on them). The front matter usually includes a half-title page, with only the title (no subtitle or author's name). It is often used for autographs. It is followed by a white page, then the recto title page, which is more comprehensive. The title page includes the title, subtitle, author's and/or editor's name, the name of the person who has written the foreword, and the publisher. It is followed by the verso page with credential information, including copyright, ISBN, Library of Congress Control Number, Cataloging in Publication data, printing history, and permissions. You also can use the verso page to give credit to the cover designers, illustrators, and others.

The verso page is followed by the dedication, a blank page, contents page(s), list of illustrations or tables (if applicable), foreword, preface, acknowledgments, and introduction. Try to start each new section on a recto page.

The foreword (not forward) should be written by some knowledgeable person *other than the author*. The preface, signed by the author if there is doubt who wrote it, includes reasons why the book was written. The introduction includes information, such as historical background, which should be read and understood before delving into the main body of the book. It is also by the author, but is unsigned. Some books may have lists of abbreviations, contributors, or a chronology.

The body of the book includes the text, which usually is divided into chapters and/or sections. Care must be taken to establish adequate margins and white space so that the pages do not look overcrowded. A rule of thumb is to have about 35 percent white space on each page. That would include the margins and the space between lines of type called leading (pronounced "ledding").

You may also want running heads or footers on the pages to identify the title of the book, chapter, topic covered on the page, or the author, and you will need to decide where you want to place the page numbers. Later in this chapter we will expand on book setup and other considerations, such as choice of type styles and sizes.

The back matter is found after the body of the book and usually includes the appendices, endnotes, glossary, bibliography or reference list, index, and perhaps a page about the author. Each section has its own specific rules, which are defined and described at length in *The Chicago Manual of Style.*

The American system of page numbering calls for the front matter and the main portion of the book to each start with the number 1. The British system begins the front matter with 1 and continues in sequence to the end. We have found that the American system is more flexible, especially if the book is to be indexed. Front matter is usually not indexed so if the number of pages of front matter changes, either while the book is being set up or in subsequent editions, it will not affect the reference page numbers in the index.

Index

All nonfiction books should be indexed. An index is extremely important to librarians and to the Library of Congress Cataloging in Publication division—to say nothing of your readers. A proper index also adds credibility to your book.

Creating an index is not as easy as it may seem, even though many computer word processing programs include an indexing function. A truly comprehensive index may require as much as an hour of work for each five pages of text, *after* the indexer has become familiar with the book. We recommend a thorough reading of the indexing section of *The Chicago Manual of Style*, and perhaps the retention of a professional indexer to do the work. Having a professional do the work is expensive, but usually worth it (see appendix A for an excellent explanation of indexing by Sandi Frank).

Your book's dimensions

In selecting the size of your book, you need to consider the following:

- Economy. Use a standard size page so that after the signatures are printed, folded and trimmed you are not wasting vast amounts of paper. Odd-size books or unusual paper stocks add significantly to the cost of producing your book.
- The size of other books dealing with the same general subject.
- The weight of your book, or its handling ease.

Mass-market paperbacks, such as pulp westerns and mysteries, and even the paperback editions of best-selling novels, can have press runs of hundreds of thousands. They are printed by web presses, like those on which newspapers are printed. The paper used, a type of newsprint, comes on huge rolls and is not readily available for small print jobs, and the dimension of those books is not the most economical size for small press runs.

The fiction and nonfiction books sold in bookstores are referred to as "trade" books. Most short-run (less than 10,000 copies) trade books are printed on sheet-fed presses, which use stacks of precut sheets of paper, much like a copy machine does. These sheets are precut in certain sizes based on the sizes of the pages commonly used in books. Using standard sizes will save money.

You usually will find that 5-by-8, 5½-by-8½, 6-by-9, or 7-by-10 inches, are the most cost-effective page sizes for trade books. These sizes conform to book standards. A coffee-table book with lots of pictures or children's books will probably be 8½-by-11 or 8-by-10 inches.

If your book is lengthy, you could consider reducing the thickness by increasing the size of the pages, changing to a lighter-weight paper, or even publishing in two volumes. You can also reduce the number of pages through font selection or leading changes, but don't sacrifice readability in the process.

Acquisition librarians and some library distributors will not purchase small-sized books, such as pocket guides; they are difficult to shelve. The 6-by-9-inch book is a standard for the library market.

Photographs and choice of paper

If you plan to have photographs in your book, try to use professional glossy prints, as they reproduce best. But, if you must use home snapshots, try to pick ones with good contrast and no busy backgrounds. Have your photographs properly cropped, sized and half-toned by a professional. The results are worth the expense. If they are to be scanned, be sure that they are scanned at the proper resolution for printing, 300 DPI, and saved in the correct format, either TIF or EPS.

Coated paper stocks, such as enamel, are much better for photo-reproduction than are the common commodity offset papers that most text-only books are printed on. They are also more expensive. Discuss your photo ideas with your packager or with your printer to determine which kind of paper is best for your job. Indicate in the text or margins approximately where the pictures should be placed. We say approximately because sometimes in the typeset version, the spot you indicate will end up in a page position that just won't fit the picture—such as a half-inch from the bottom of the page. Give your typesetter some leeway in picture placement.

You will need to write a short cutline for each photograph. A cutline, or caption, should tell the picture's story and identify the people in the picture from left to right. Don't retell the text in the caption.

Types of bindings and cover materials

Most books that you see on bookstore shelves are bound with what is known as a perfect binding. Perfect binding is accomplished by gathering the signatures, trimming off the spine or gutter area, then gluing a paper cover directly to the body of the book. A signature is a group of pages printed on both sides of one flat sheet that has been folded and trimmed. The number of pages in a signature is commonly a multiple of eight, and will depend on the dimensions of the book and the size of the press. Perfect binding has a squared-off look and is quite economical. This book has a perfect binding.

Perfect-bound books usually are simply glued together, but sometimes are smyth sewn, a process in which the signatures are stitched together with strong nylon thread for added durability. Casebound, or hardcover books, are almost always smyth sewn.

Pamphlets, small guidebooks or other books with fewer than fifty pages or so usually have a saddlestitch binding. The cover is folded around the text, then stapled or stitched to the pages. The signatures are trimmed top and bottom and outside but not on the spine.

Gene Starner evaluates a book's binding when he selects regional titles for the Barnes & Noble's stores: "Perfect binding is more expensive [than saddlestitching], but perfect-bound books have the potential for a longer shelf life and better sales because the name of the book can be placed on the spine. Since most of our books are placed on the shelves spine out, stapled or saddlestitched books essentially disappear. Also, many of our stores are not carrying stapled books unless they come with a shelf or counter display."

 If your book will be sold or stored where there is high humidity, you should specify that the cover be coated with a lay-flat treatment.

A hardcover or case binding will add considerably to the cost per copy of your book. If you have a hardcover you will usually need to have a dust jacket made for it. Bookstores like dust jackets because if there is damage, it is more economical to replace a jacket than an entire book, but dust jackets are expensive, especially if they are printed with four colors.

Some casebound books, such as children's books, textbooks, or coffee-table books, may have the cover design printed on the finished case. Others have a foil-stamped cloth or plastic over the binder board.

There are many types of cover materials to select from for either hardbound or softcover books. Check bookstores and libraries to see what material books of your kind use. Most paperback cover stock is 9-, 10- or 12-point and coated on one or two sides to help prevent curling. After printing, the cover is treated with film lamination, UV coating, or varnish to make it glossy and to protect it.

Although the type of binding you select may be based on how much you have to invest in your book, you also need to consider how it will be used. Cookbooks, for instance, are handier if they have a washable cover and lie flat. Many are bound with a plastic spiral binding, which is also called a comb or GBC binding, but bookstores find this type of binding difficult to store and display, and libraries don't like books with spiral bindings.

Otabind is a type of perfect binding that is designed to open and lie flat on the reading surface. The cover is not glued to the book's spine, allowing the cover to bend freely. This type of cover is good for cookbooks, how-to, and music books—where pages need to stay open while the reader's hands are occupied. One of our favorite cookbooks, *Simply Whidbey: A collection of regional recipes from Whidbey Island, Washington,* by Laura Moore and Deborah Skinner, is a an example of the usefulness of the lay-flat cover. Musician/composer Adam Cole also chose a lay-flat cover for his *Ballet Music for the Dance Accompanist,* so it would stay open on a piano. Fishing and cruising guidebooks, and other books that are meant to be used outdoors, might hold up better if they were printed on waterproof stock. It is available, but expensive.

Fonts

Your book packager, typesetter, or desktop publishing program will have many standard fonts, or typefaces, available to use for the body text of your book. You should choose one that has serifs (the little hooks on each letter) rather than a sans serif font (without the little hooks), such as those often used in newsletters or advertising. Serif fonts are much easier to read:

New Century Schoolbook has serifs!

Classical Sans does not!

Sans serif fonts, such as Classical Sans, are OK for use as chapter or section heads, and in cover design or advertising copy, but in text they are tiresome to read because there are no serifs to lead the reader's eye along the sentence. Don't use a sans serif font for the text.

Make sure that type size fits your potential readership. Books for older eyes and for young children use a larger point size than those used for the average adult.

Type size is measured in points. Each point equals $\frac{1}{72}$ of an inch. Books commonly use type that is 10, 11, or maybe even 12 point. In this book we have used 11-point Times for the body text. Over the length of a book, the font selection can make a considerable difference in the number of pages.

Here are some common book fonts. Notice the slight difference in the length of the first three words used in these samples:

This font is   New Baskerville.

This font is   Garamond.

This font is   Bookman.

This font is   Times.

This font is   Palatino.

All of the above sample fonts are 11 point but, as you can see, they will each result in a different length to your book and may impact the cost of production. If we had wanted this book to be longer, perhaps to reach an even signature break, we might have used New Baskerville or Garamond.

The next examples of text, all in one font, show how the point size can affect the length and readability of a sentence. Be sure you select your font to fit your readers' age and eyesight.

This is Garamond 9 point.

This is Garamond 10 point.

This is Garamond 11 point.

This is Garamond 12 point.

As you can see, the typeface and point size each, or in combination, can have an appreciable effect on the overall size of your book and its readability. If you are not working with a packager or professional book typesetter, carefully study the fonts used in mainstream books so your choice will be appropriate to the type of book you are producing and the age of the reader.

If you are going to prepare your own electronic files for a book manufacturer, try to use PostScript fonts. Your computer probably came with TrueType fonts, but these often will not work properly with the equipment the book manufacturers use to produce the film or the plates. TrueType fonts are a sort of "shadow," or "ghost," of a font, an abbreviation if you will. Unfortunately, technical output equipment sometimes does not recognize them and will default to Courier. They are fine, however, for creating camera-ready copy.

Another problem, which can rear its ugly head when using a word-processing program to create your files, is that of bitmapping. A bitmap file is one where the graphics image or text is formed by a pattern of dots. These low-resolution images are sometimes called paint-type images and usually have a lower number of dots per inch than the high-resolution text or images needed for printing. The examples below clearly show the differences in print output between a bitmapped image and one created using a high-end page design program.

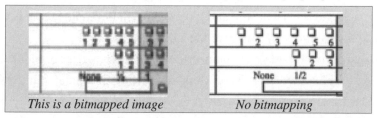

| *This is a bitmapped image* | *No bitmapping* |

Remember that leading is also important. Too much space between the lines of type makes the eye lose contact while searching for the next line, and reading loses its flow. If the lines are too close together, they are hard to read. The leading used in this book is 16-point or about 139 percent of the point size of the typeface. The leading for trade fiction is often greater than 130 percent. In mass market books or magazines it is usually 120 percent.

The combination of typesetting, white space, and leading contributes to the elegance of a book. If you want to become more knowledgeable about typography and graphics, there are many good resources available.

Writer Robin Williams lists thirteen telltale signs of do-it-yourself desktop publishing. The way you use type, indentations, underlining, caps, spacing after periods, and gray boxes will expose your book as an amateur product. Williams concludes: "Creating professional-level type is simply a matter of becoming more aware of details. It doesn't take any more time to do it right, and these details are certainly not difficult to gain control over."[14] Her books, *Non-Designer's Design Book* and *A Blip in the Continuum,* share more secrets of typography and graphic design.

Technology considerations

In what form will a packager or typesetter want your manuscript? So far we have talked about the many essential style elements of your book. The technology available to produce the guts of your book is also important. You need to be aware of the best and least expensive ways to provide your packager or typesetter with your manuscript.

If your manuscript is handwritten you will have no choice but to have it typed into a word processing program that is compatible with your packager's page design and typesetting program. Retyping is time-consuming and costly, but it is the only alternative.

If you have typed your manuscript using a typewriter or older word processor, you may have two options for getting it translated into print.

The first, as with handwritten copy, is to have it retyped by hand into your typesetter or packager's program. This is usually the most labor-intensive and most costly option.

The second alternative is to have the pages scanned by an optical scanner with a good OCR (optical character recognition) program. Your packager or typesetter should have one in his armory of equipment. Scanning may be less costly than retyping, but works well only if your copy is extremely clean. That means that if your ribbon is old, if the keys of the typewriter need cleaning or if you have a dot-matrix printer for your word processor, your letter "o" may be read by the scanner as an "a." Your letter "I" may be read as a number 1. Scanner-created typos produce another of those technical problems that take time to fix, and time is money. Scanning does not pick up handwritten notes or corrections, so if your manuscript is full of editorial notes or corrections you are a candidate for a retype rather than a scan.

Scanning or typing costs can vary considerably, depending on where you have it done and what type of equipment is used.

For most serious writers, though, home computers and word processors are now more common than old-fashioned typewriters or a pencil and a legal pad.

Although computers make your work easier, sometimes they also can create headaches, especially for your typesetter or packager. The use of obscure programs or old systems that are no longer compatible with modern standards will make the jobs of editing and typesetting more difficult.

You need to let your typesetter or book packager know in what form your manuscript is coming and, if on disk, what system and program was used. They will need to know whether the system is IBM-compatible, Macintosh or a word processor. Most word processors, and many obsolete early computer systems such as Commodore and Kaypro, are not compatible with modern computers. Their technology has been passed by and forgotten by the modern computer industry. You are likely save money and time by converting your material to your typesetter's or packager's system.

Virtually any attempt by authors, however well-meaning, to format inside pages, will most likely end up being work that must be undone by editors and the typesetter. Certain codes, like tabs and carriage returns, will not be overridden by the styles your typesetter applies. They will have to be deleted individually, and that means more time that you will have to pay for. Try to resist the urge to try to make your draft look like a finished book in your own computer program. Just type the manuscript into your computer without fancy formats.

All the time you spend making your work look "like a book" will confuse the program into which your work will be converted. Then it will take more of the typesetter's time because he or she will have to go through the files and delete all the formatting you put in.

The easier you make the job for the person you are hiring, the more you will be able to save on the project. If the programs are compatible, your book can be worked on by directly importing the text from your disk.

There are many good word processing programs that are easy to use, such as MSWord from Microsoft, AmiPro from Lotus, and WordPerfect from Corel.

These programs all have spell-checking programs, find-and-replace features, and block-editing capabilities that make it easy for you to work with your copy. Keep in mind that a computer spell check is no substitute for proofreading. For example, the spelling programs will recognize that "there," "they're," and "their" are all spelled correctly, but will not flag which is appropriate in the context of the sentence.

Another advantage of using a computer is that you can deliver your book on disk, rather than as a pile of hard copy.

Just as there is a big difference between printers and publishers, there is a big difference between setting up camera-ready pages using an ordinary word processing program, versus a typesetting program such as Adobe PageMaker, InDesign or Quark Express.

Many self-published books are produced by authors using word-processing programs. Unfortunately, despite the ability to use a good book typeface to generate their camera-ready copy or PDF files, their work may still end up looking less than professional without the page design and typesetting techniques that a quality typesetter can provide. For example, text needs to be balanced on pages. You need to avoid widows and orphans—the first or last sentence of a paragraph hanging alone at the top or bottom of a page or column. Letters often need to be kerned (spaced aesthetically) and the leading must be adjusted. These are important details for your professional book typesetter, and for the proper look of your book.

If you are generating your own camera-ready copy on a laser printer, make sure that the resolution is at least 600 dpi (dots per inch), preferably more. Most personal (home or office) laser or ink-jet printers, including those at quick print shops, produce only 300 or 360 dpi copy. Many ink-jet printers produce splatter not easily visible to the eye, but obvious in the printed copy. Some of the newer laser and better ink-jet printers generate copy at 600 dpi or even higher. At lower resolutions the letters and graphics will not be as sharply defined and the finished product will not look as good as it should, especially to the practiced eyes of the wholesale buyers. If you are using a packager or are having your camera-ready text generated by a service bureau, the resolution should be much higher to conform to industry standards. Professional image setters produce copy at 2,400 dpi.

The camera-ready copy for the first edition of this book was produced at 1,200 dpi on a LaserMaster Unity 1200 LX-0 typesetter. The second edition on an 1,800 dpi model. The press-ready copy for this edition was sent on a CD as a Press-Ready PDF (portable document format) created at 2,400 dpi.

According to typesetter Bob Lefebvre, "The formatting of a book is vastly different than that of any other printed product. Most desktop publishers shy away from this type of project due to their lack of knowledge concerning the anatomy of a book. Acceptable margins, text positioning, and the sequencing of sections are very precise elements. The professionalism of your finished product—your book—is all in the details."

Submitting on disk

Most book manufacturers now accept your copy on floppy disk or CD, then do the prepress work electronically. If you have the equipment and programs to submit your work this way, be sure to work closely with your book manufacturer—*before* you format the final disk to be sure you do the setup work correctly. Unless you adhere to strict instructions about which files to include on your disk, and what format to have them in, there are no guarantees that what you have seen on your screen or on your draft copy will look the same when you get your galley proofs from the printer.

If you have not included all your font files, the printer's system will usually substitute the default font (usually `Courier`), for yours, and all the careful work you have done formatting your pages will be for naught. If you have placed images in your book, it is necessary that you include the original scans on the disk or CD also.

The arguments for submitting on disk include quicker turnaround, cost savings, and high-resolution output—with Adobe Acrobat PDF submission you can output press-optimized files at 2,400 dpi.

There are some advantages to this process. Submitting the book on disk eliminates shooting the film from laser-printed, camera-ready copy, where sometimes the toner literally falls off the page or may crack, leaving little breaks in letters or words. And, ink-jet printers produce splatter that is invisible to the eye, but can cause the final print output to be a bit fuzzy. Some book manufacturers offer a discount to publishers who submit their books on disk, others now charge a surcharge if you send your work as camera-ready.

Your book—cover, text, illustrations, and photographs—can also be submitted on disk or CD to a print-on-demand company.

5 Promoting your book

Enthusiasm for books is what sells books.
—Fred Ciporen, publisher, *Publishers Weekly*[15]

We have said this before, but we can't emphasize it enough—you may think of your book as a work of art, and it is, but when printed in quantity, your book is a product. Like all retail products, it must be professionally produced, and effectively promoted and marketed. Most products will not sell if they are not promoted. Your book will be best promoted through your own determination and diligent effort.

If you are the shy type (many of us started out that way) who absolutely freezes in public and would rather clean the cat box than greet strangers, you better make sure you have a creative marketing program and money set aside to put into an advertising campaign. If you don't, you may end up with a garage full of wonderful books to leave to your heirs.

The point at which the delivery truck arrives at your door or storage unit may be the point at which you and your team of professionals or book packager part company, depending on your agreement with them. Some packagers have marketing services you can contract for once the setup and production phases are completed. Others will guide you to marketing or publicity people. A few may even help you get launched as part of their deal with you. Discuss your arrangements well ahead of your delivery date, so you can prepare your game plan.

Remember, though, the ultimate success of marketing and sales will rest on your shoulders—you, the publisher.

Keep in mind that market research is finding what customers want and filling their need, but you must have publicity to let the public know about what you have to sell them. Once you know who the most likely customers are for your book, then you have to let them know the book is available. You can toot your own horn any number of ways. Some methods cost money, but some 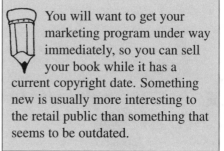 You will want to get your marketing program under way immediately, so you can sell your book while it has a current copyright date. Something new is usually more interesting to the retail public than something that seems to be outdated.

don't. Make the most of the free ones! Remember, any costs you incur for marketing need to be prorated to a cost-per-copy basis and added to your production costs. You should at least mentally review these costs early on so you can adjust your retail price and size of press run to accommodate them.

Reviews

There are two types of reviewers, each serving different categories of book buyers.

First, there are those who review for the book trade: *Publishers Weekly, Library Journal, ForeWord, Independent Publisher Online, Booklist*, and *Kirkus Review,* among others. These publications review forthcoming books shortly before their publication for those who own and manage bookstores, libraries, wholesalers and distributors.

The second category are reviewers for the retail consumer—the folks who will go to the bookstore, library, or Internet to buy or read books. These reviews are published in major newspapers, such as the *New York Times;* specialty magazines, such as automotive or entertainment; and local, regional or national media. Or they may be found on Internet sites.

You will need to decide well before your book is released if you want to try to be reviewed nationally. If so, you probably will need to have bound galleys (sometimes called "Cranes" after the company that first printed them) made to submit to reviewers who require them. Bound galleys are made from a set of your early, uncorrected page proofs. They used to be most often bound with an inexpensive cardstock printed cover, but many publishers are sending a color prototype of the cover or the dust jacket with the bound galleys. Print-on-demand companies can prepare bound galleys for you (see appendix resource list). Many reviewers like to see what the cover will look like.

Denny Fried, who coauthored *Memoirs of a Papillon: The Canine Guide to Living with Humans* with his charming four-legged companion, Genevieve, received excellent national reviews including one from *ForeWord* magazine, as his book came off press. The reviews gave him a boost in the retail market, but he didn't rest on his laurels. He ran monthly ads in *Radio and TV Interview Report*, and quickly garnered twenty radio and television interviews. While he could not directly attach sales to the interviews, Fried said, "The value for me is that I call all bookstores within range of the stations and in almost every case they are happy to have me bring in books if they don't already stock it." And the interviews have helped him get into additional chain stores.

Part of his marketing strategy is to have Genevieve, and his wife, Katrina, with him as they promote the book. "Genevieve, as corporate spokesdog, is a magical draw, something few authors have in their book promotion," he said. She is the life of every autographing party and is selling books faster than you can chase a ball.

Genevieve also has a regular column on the Internet site, www.e-fido.net, and a link brings readers back to the Eiffel Press site, www.gvieve.com, for book sales.

Fried understands the power of having a high quality product, a dynamite cover, national reviews, and relentless promotion in bookstores and on the Web. Within two years, he sold more than 20,000 copies in four printings. For some of his insights, see appendix B.

The cover of a bound galley is different from the cover of the final book. It should specify the title, author, author's biographical information, your publication date, price, ISBN, number of pages and illustrations, first printing figures, and your anticipated advertising and promotion budget, plus rights sale information. This information is often printed on the back cover. On the front cover print "uncorrected page proofs" or "advance reading edition."

Those who review for the trade generally want to see the bound galleys or uncorrected page proofs three to four months *before* the planned publication date. That way, book buyers can read the review and place orders so that it is in stock on the publication date. They can then take advantage of the marketing hype and publicity.

Those who review for the consumer are not always as concerned with the time frame of the review because the book needs to be available for purchase when the review comes out. They will want to see the finished product just before or at least shortly after the release date. Sometimes they will accept an advance reader edition, which is substantively complete but not finally proofed. Publishers at book trade shows often give out copies of the uncorrected advance reader editions instead of a completed book.

Remember that there are thousands of new books published each year and, although only a small percentage are submitted for review, your book will need to stand out to be considered. *Publishers Weekly* alone receives more than six hundred titles a week for consideration in its *Library Journal*.

Call the editors of the publications for current policies for reviews, but do not be discouraged that larger papers don't have space for reviews. Small press and local books are competing for review space with the national best-sellers, and many book-page editors find it's less problematic for them to critique the "safe" books—the ones that have already been reviewed by other sources—than to chance an unknown author. Reviewers at medium-sized papers (a circulation of less than 200,000) may receive hundreds of books a week—unsolicited—from large and small presses. The homemade-looking books are quickly put aside—a good reason to make every effort for your book to be professional in every detail. One newspaper book reviewer told us that because she believes that cookbooks will be more likely to be discussed in the lifestyle section, and religious books may catch the eye of the religion editor, she limits her consideration to books of very general interest. And then she is further guided by national book promotion for books that will appeal to most readers.

You may send your bound galleys to *Publishers Weekly, Literary Marketplace, Library Journal, Kirkus Review, New York Times Book Review, ForeWord, Independent Publisher Online,* and *ALA Booklist.*

Selection process for pre-pub galleys

One review editor receives six hundred books a month and, in addition, scans publishers' catalogs for worthy titles to request for review. Ninety-eight percent of the galleys are from independent and university publishers. Forty-five galleys are chosen.

The galley cover is seen first. Most galleys have covers that are merely fact sheets with title, subtitle, author, illustrations, binding, price, pages, category, ISBN, pub date and contact name. There also are galleys that have a version of the cover art that will appear on the book; these galleys attract more attention than the others. If the title and subtitle are understood and interesting then the content is considered.

Is the content new, different, or worthwhile? The accompanying press release or fact sheet provides a summary highlighting the benefits of the book or its reason for publication. After reading this information the review editor scans the galley and decides whether the content is worthwhile for libraries and booksellers. If it is worthwhile, the review editor then considers whether the book will be more valuable than other worthwhile books. There are several factors to be considered in light of the review publication's next issue: when was a book by this publisher last reviewed, is the subject already represented in the category for the next issue, is there a noteworthy event that coincides with the book's publication, is the subject matter representative of an important trend, does the content coincide with the editorial calendar, is there a significant audience, is the author noteworthy, etc. The answers are determined and a decision quickly made because of the volume of galleys received. The review editor then selects the best reviewers for the galleys chosen.

If the galley is from a self-publisher, that publisher's name should appear credible, e.g., Two Squirrels Press appears less credible than a name like Stanford Press or Parthenon House. The design and layout of the galley are then looked at for credibility. The text layout with an amateur desktop publisher look is usually less credible than a design that mimics a Random House or Simon & Schuster. Professional book packagers usually follow the traditional style or a style that complements content to exude believability. Finally, the content is considered. These factors are of concern because the credibility of the review publication itself is important.

—Alex Moore, review editor, *ForeWord* magazine

One review source, *Independent Publisher Online*, will consider finished nonfiction published within the current calendar year; *Foreword* prefers books or galleys four months prior to publication. *Bas Bleu* and *Common Reader* are book catalogs that review books they carry.

A review by any of these major trade publications can be extremely beneficial. *Booklist,* for instance, is a guide to current print and non-print materials considered worthy of purchase by small and medium-sized public libraries and school library media centers. A review in *Booklist* constitutes a recommendation for purchase by libraries, according to the American Library Association.

Target your review sources carefully rather than randomly sending out copies. You might even contact the reviewers first to determine if they are interested in seeing your book.

Even if a newspaper or magazine does not have a book review section, you can sometimes interest an appropriate editor or writer (business, medical, sports, religion, or features) in writing about you and your book. Some of the best press coverage for books we have seen has come through the feature writers.

And, don't forget about radio or television reviews, or maybe even an interview. Millions of people listen to "Fresh Air" on National Public Radio. "Morning Edition" discusses books, as does "Weekend Edition." You might send your book to news magazines, such as *U.S. News & World Report, Time, Newsweek,* and even the Sunday supplement, *Parade* magazine— if your book has a national audience.

When Oprah Winfrey had her monthly book club, a mention could mean an instant 50,000 copies sold. Competition was stiff for her picks and publishers whose books were selected had to able

Send a press release with your bound galley or review copy. The press release should include pertinent information, such as: The price, ISBN, author, illustrator, story summary, number of pages (even if it is an estimate) type of binding, anticipated publication date, other books the author has written, awards, and advance praise or blurbs, if any. You will make the reviewer's job much easier, and some of the information may find its way into the review or article.

to deliver the copies to their wholesaler before she announced her selection. Keep that in mind if you are seeking national talk show exposure. Most self-publishers would not be advised to have that large a press run, especially on speculation. Before you get your hopes up or spend a fortune on blindly mailing review copies around the globe, analyze which media targets may be viable based on the books they typically review. If a radio or TV host is only interested in sports, don't send your teen romance or children's book to him or her.

There are also opportunities for book reviews in many specialty magazines and professional journals. If you have a religious topic or a human interest story with a religious twist, you might look toward church newsletters for advertising or reviews.

Depending on your subject, and the professionalism of your product, you might be fortunate enough to attract national attention. Realistically, don't expect to be reviewed by the traditional media sources like the Big Guys often are, and don't pin your marketing plans on being reviewed. The giant

Become familiar with all of the newspapers in your region before sending out review copies. Find out:

1. If reviews are done, and who does them.
2. Which writers, freelancers or columnists might be interested in your topic

Don't mention that your book is self-published in your publicity material. Newspaper people generally are book snobs. They don't understand the changing world of publishing and often think, because they have seen so many poorly produced ones, that self-published books are automatically no good.

publishing houses sink hundreds of thousands of dollars into media campaigns, even to the extent of "buying" the covers of major trade magazines as advertisements to catch the attention of reviewers and bookstores. The hype works, and often the books sell, no matter what the quality of the material. Authors who have been reviewed are more likely to be reviewed again, especially if the first book had moderate success.

If your book does not get reviewed, and it is likely that it won't be, you might consider calling the reviewers to try to learn just why it

Tom Coughlin, a certified public accountant living in Manchester, New Hampshire, wrote a steamy romance, *Maggie May's Diary*, featuring a female CPA, and a lot of place-name dropping. His strategy earned him strong sales in New Hampshire and coastal Maine and in less than a year, he ordered a second printing. He was also the subject of a major feature story in a regional edition of the *Boston Globe*. As an unknown author, Coughlin had been having difficulty getting the attention of reviewers or writers at the *Globe,* so he contacted freelance feature writer Mark Dagostino. Dagostino became interested in Coughlin's marketing strategy of mentioning the names of towns in Maine, where he has a summer home, and in the Manchester area. In his lengthy article about Coughlin and the book, Dagostino noted that other writers, such as Stephen King and John Irving, had also set their fiction in familiar places. Coughlin and a copy of *Maggie May's Diary* were photographed on a beach and the large picture was printed on the section front with the beginning of the article. Coughlin was quoted as saying that tourists visiting the southern coast of Maine would be able to read about the very beach on which they are walking. Dagostino got comments from bookstore owners about why they liked the book's local touch.

He interviewed Coughlin about writing the book, and gave a positive explanation for why an author would self-publish.

Coughlin does not rely on that one major feature story in the *Globe* to sustain sales of his book. He regularly visits bookstores, independents and chains, and schedules signings to keep his name and book visible. When he published *Brian Kelly: Route 1,* the prequel to *Maggie May's Diary* in the summer of 2001, he had advance orders for several thousand copies from stores that had been enjoying steady sales from his first book. Meanwhile, his lifelong dream of being a writer—and a successful one at that—has been realized.

wasn't accepted for review. It might have been that there were a number of books about the same subject, or it might have been that your cover looked amateurish. Listen carefully to the answer so that you profit another time from their advice.

We also suggest concentrating your efforts locally, or at least begin in an area with a radius of a half-day drive, and taking advantage of all available publicity within your local market. If these efforts are successful, then begin to expand your marketing area.

Newspapers

A basic assumption of this book is that you will try to sell as many books as possible in your own community or region, where people that you know, and who know you, live. That's also where you know, or build a relationship with, the booksellers and the media folks. And don't forget the gift and card shops—any place that carries books. You also need to know who does what at the newspaper, and what the special section deadlines are. Ask how much lead time the editor needs if you want the information in the paper's calendar of events, announcement section, or in the book signing section (the Sunday editions of some papers have them). You need to ask for the names of writers or editors who should receive a copy of your press release, because different people may be assigned to each of those details. Ask if someone at the paper writes reviews, or who might write a feature.

Make sure that if you part with a review copy, it has a real chance of being reviewed or will at least receive coverage. Most local papers do not do book reviews *per se*, but sometimes you can get a feature story about the book, especially if you emphasize a local angle.

Realities of the "book page"

As we noted earlier, book page editors at larger metropolitan papers may receive hundreds of books a week. Yes, a *week*. You can tell who the book editors are by their hands—bloodied from opening mailing envelopes and dealing with staples and box cutters. No book page editor has time to read that many books, so a quick sorting is made, and those that qualify for a possible mention are set aside. The rest—maybe 175 of them—are given away to co-workers or to local libraries and reading programs. The books that *look* self-published are usually the first to hit the giveaway pile.

Of those chosen for a closer look, only a few will make it to the book page. Usually they are ones already being featured by other national review sources. Often book editors will wait to see what other reviewers have to say, and may well take a review that is available from the wire services rather than write their own.

Although many book editors would like to read as many new books as possible, we knew at least one editor who only read literary classics and would not consider reading a book by a contemporary author unless she were left on a desert island with no other option.

Tell your story

Once you have been publicized, readers will begin to ask for your book at the bookstores or the library, and that is the name of the game. In your press releases, publicize the names of the retail outlets where your book is available and the phone number for your distributor or fulfillment house.

Remember, in the overall scheme of things at a daily paper, a press release about the publication of a new book or a book signing is very seldom the top story of the day. Try to tie your release into an event that is worthy of a news announcement to give the media a reason to use it. Be patient if your story or press release doesn't appear immediately. But, if several weeks go by and you still haven't seen the story, there is nothing wrong with calling to find out if the press release was received, or if the writer or reporter needs additional information to complete the story. If you have a fax machine—wonderful for distributing press releases—send another copy. E-mail can land you at the right person's desk at a paper. Be sure to direct it to the specific writer or desk, such as religion, food, sports, or features, that will deal with the information. Your press release should include the name and phone number of someone who may be contacted for more information, and that person's title (author, publisher). Describe the activity you have planned in conjunction with the book signing. James Kaserman, author of *Gasparilla: Pirate Genius*, and a teen version, *The Legend of Gasparilla: A Tale for All Ages,* dresses in a pirate costume for book signings. His wife, Jane, co-author of the second book, also appears in costume and plays period music on her violin, drawing a crowd, and sometimes news photographers or TV cameras.

Many Sunday papers have a place for book signing and author event announcements on the book page. Send in your brief announce-

Author Tom Grimshaw's *In Like a Lamb . . . Out Like a Lion* has received excellent reviews from magazines that cover car racing. The book's account of the incredible driving career of John Buffum, America's most famous rally race car driver, was reviewed by Andrew Bornhop in *Road and Track* magazine. Grimshaw, a gifted writer, served as Buffum's codriver throughout the peak of his career, giving him special biographical insight. The reviews in magazines that cater to a specific audience have produced orders from bookstores and readers around the country.

ment ten days to two weeks before the calendar is published so that you can get maximum free publicity. It is a good way to let people know about your book, even if they don't come to the signing. Sometimes the bookstore hosting your event will include details about the signing in its monthly community calendar and will distribute the calendar to the local media. But, don't count on the store's calendar making it into the newspaper's Sunday or weekday calendars. Always do your own publicity rather than relying on the store to generate it.

 Speaking of giving away copies of your book to reviewers, you will discover that many people you know (and some you don't) will have their hands out for a free copy. Sometimes they are very brazen. Make a list of the people to whom you want to give a copy, then be ready to remind all your "new best friends" that publishing is a business and your book is a product. They either can purchase the book at the bookstore or from you—perhaps at a special discount.

Negative press

To a point, bad press or negative reviews are better than none at all. People may not remember the details of an article, but they might remember the title or topic, and buy the book later. Most books banned in Boston have enjoyed good sales (especially, in Boston).

If you have produced a quality product, you will avoid reviewers' criticism of the editing, production, veracity of jacket claims about the book, or documentation of material, rather than writing about the merits of your book. An example of the type of criticism you do not want appeared in *The White Tops* magazine (March/April 2000) about a book that had good information about the circus and was otherwise interesting. The reviewer said that the fault of the book was "sloppiness in the publishing process. Unfortunately this is a common failure these days in books that are prepared through desktop publishing. Nobody bothers to make sure the punctuation is correct, style is consistent, proper names are capitalized . . . the basics of putting words on paper."

Most reviewers would probably not bother reading or writing about a "sloppy" book. However, they will pick at inaccuracies. Louis Menard, writing in the *New Yorker*,[16] took two books to task in a review, the first for its misleading title, and the second for its misleading jacket. He said *The Concise Book of Lying* "is not concise" and that *The Liar's Tale: A History of Falsehood* "is not a history of falsehood, or, for that matter, the tale of a liar." He goes on to say that while the author (these are not self-published books) is not considered responsible for promotional material printed on the jacket, there is a "falsehood" on the jacket relating to what the book is about. The error obviously grates and adds to the reviewer's rant about merits of the book. As self-publishers, exercising perhaps more control than authors of books purchased by publishing houses, you can avoid these problems by carefully choosing your titles and the wording of promotional materials.

So what should you do if you get a bad review? Don't berate newspaper writers or reviewers if you disagree with their point of view or if there is a mistake in their article. It's OK to ask for a *correction* (not a *retraction*) if there is a glaring factual error, such as your phone number. If the errors are minor, just suggest pleasantly, "In the future, please correct the following information: —"

It is astonishing how wrong information, such as the book's title or your name, can appear in print, even when a reporter or clerk has correct material in front of them. It's best to phrase your request for corrections nicely. You do *not* want to make enemies of the media. Clerks, reporters, and editors don't err on purpose, and you may need them later to publicize your signings or other newsworthy events. And be sure to thank them after a story has run. It's surprising how few people do. There's nothing wrong with thanking a reviewer who has seen only a bound galley for a nice review by sending a note and a copy of the finished book.

Advertising that works

If you decide to place print ads, make sure you place them in the magazines or newspapers that will reach your market. For example, if you have written about World War II, consider advertising in veterans' magazines. If you have written a book of poetry, perhaps advertise it in a literary magazine. An advertisement in a specialty magazine may lead to a review, especially if you send a complimentary copy to the features writer by name.

Print advertising is expensive; certainly you can't afford to advertise in every magazine or directory. Be selective in your choices and make your ads work for you. Some advertising publications will give you "free editorial" space if you purchase an ad. You might be able to write a regular column in some magazines, if the publication reaches your target market, for the price of an ad.

 Put the most important information in the first two or three paragraphs of your press release.

Try including coupons or special offers so you can track the effectiveness of your ads in various media. If you make each offer and/or coupon different, you will be able to track results to see which publications are best for you. The replies you receive should become the basis for a mailing list. However, if you are giving your message to the wrong market, or the wrong message to the right market, you may receive hundreds of replies asking for free information—but no actual sales. For example, advertising book-packaging services for self-publishing authors in a magazine that caters to writers seeking rights-buying publishers is targeting the wrong market. We know.

Including a testimonial or quote about your book or its topic can be compelling. For advertising purposes, put your selling point in quotes: "Congratulations on your success with *Smart Self-Publishing*. A lot of books come out on this topic, and yours seems to have joined the select few that are widely considered to be musts for the professional libraries of new publishers." Steve Carlson, *Big Books from Small Presses.*

Avoid having a headline in your ad that asks any question that can be answered, "No." You will be giving your customer an excuse for not buying your book. Power statements such as, "Learn How to Get Rich!" or, "Ten Easy Steps to Popularity" set a positive tone and are much more likely to result in sales.

Writing effective press releases

There are two people to keep in mind when you are writing your press release. The first is the person at the newspaper (radio station, magazine, television station, or book reviewer) who will read it and decide whether, when, and how it will be used. The second is the reader you ultimately want to reach. Here are some essentials:

- Use publisher letterhead and include your address, phone number, fax number and e-mail address, if you have them.
- Focus your release on what makes the information newsworthy.
- Include the date you sent the release or when it can be used.
- Emphasize what is special about the book and author's credentials in the subject or ties to the area.
- Tailor your basic press release to a given market by changing the first paragraph or two.
- Keep the length of your press release to a page if possible.
- Include the title and subtitle of your book as well as pertinent information: publisher, price, number of pages, ordering information, and number of photographs.
- Think about the selling points of your book. Why should people want to buy it? Will it help them solve a problem or make them rich?
- Decide if focusing on the author is a selling point. That isn't always the case. If the author is an expert in the field or has wide name recognition, capitalize on that.
- Offer to send a review copy if the reviewer wants one, and enclose a pre-stamped and addressed request card for them to mail to you.

Some hometown papers will use a press release because the author is local, but papers in larger metropolitan areas need more reason

Here's an example of how to pack information into a press release.

to include even a brief mention in a book section. Keep in mind that the book is a product and you must make consumers want to buy it. Make your press release interesting enough that the newspaper feels it is newsworthy. What are the book's features and benefits?

There are public relations companies that will write and distribute camera-ready, feature-length newspaper articles and fillers about non-fiction titles to small newspapers and shopping guides around the country. Some smaller or weekly papers will simply import the prefab article directly to their page. If you are not good at writing short articles, this may be an avenue to explore. There are a growing number of Internet companies that distribute electronic press releases.

> If your book jacket or cover is designed and worded correctly, you can recycle that information into your advertisements and press releases.

Newspaper staff edits articles, stories and press releases to fit the available space. As you write your release or article, study it from this point of view: If an editor cuts my release from the bottom up, will the essential facts still be included?

Don't expect editors or news clerks to spend time rewriting your release. You will have a much better chance of having your material used if you do it right. If you send out a longer press release, you may include more information on the author

> Don't schedule book signings or other promotional events until you have the books in hand! Many an author has had to back out of a signing commitment because of a printing delay or delivery problem. It is not only an embarrassing situation, but valuable publicity is lost.

(always write about yourself in the third person) and more details from the book. But you can see in the sample release on p. 91, we have included the news "peg" (the book signing—including the who, what, why, when, and where—all in the first few paragraphs), a little of what the book is about, its cost, its cover and where to get more information about it. You should put the name of your book or publishing house and a page number in one of the upper corners, especially if the pages of the release are not stapled. At the bottom of the first page, and each subsequent page except the last, write "more" in parenthesis. The -30- or ### symbol tells editors they have reached the end of your release and haven't lost a page on their desk.

Great gift for Mom!
Kippie Martin to autograph
Superwoman does NOT exist
Here on Friday, (date)
2-4 P.M.

File your press releases in the memory of your computer or word processor so that you can quickly retrieve and modify them to reflect critical reviews, new book signings, or awards, or to tailor them for a specific audience. If your book is more readily available through you (the publisher) or a fulfillment house than it is through bookstores, include the cost of shipping and sales tax, plus an address, or preferably the 800 number, of your fulfillment house in your release.

In the section on newspapers, we have included more about how to write and modify press releases, but here is why doing so is important. When Jim Robertson developed his press releases for *TeleVisionaries,* he customized the lead (first sentence) to whichever part of the country it was being sent to promote his experience at public television stations there. The author information was a selling point in this instance because of his role as a founder of public television stations in several cities. The local connection gave the regional newspapers a reason to do a story or give the book a mention.

Mary Ereth, a retired elementary-school teacher, and her husband became puppy-raisers for the Southeast Guide Dog Association. They decided to document their experiences with CJ, a sweet, yellow Labrador retriever, during the year that they raised her. As part of the training, the Ereths and CJ visited schools, nursing homes, and restaurants, making many friends as the pup was learning the basics of behavior. One of those friends was newspaper editor Tammy Patzer, who wrote periodically about the raising of CJ. And Tammy was only too happy to remind her readers that Mary was writing a charming book, which was illustrated with color photographs taken that year.

By the time the book was off press, just before the holidays Mary had a number of book signings lined up—some at bookstores, others at less conventional locations, such as pet shops, street fairs, veterinarian offices and the art guild. Thanks to publicity from local papers, and an already well established interest in Mary and CJ, the book sold faster than a dog can shred a morning paper. She often sold more than fifty copies at a time.

"One lady had me sign a book and write a note for her daughter's dog—a yellow Lab male named Riley, who has CJ's picture on the refrig at his sight level since summer," Ereth said.

Ereth's press releases encouraged people to bring their cameras so they could be photographed with CJ—a real crowd-pleaser that didn't cost the author or store anything.

She has since written another book, this one for the Animal Welfare League called *A New Leash on Life: An Owner's Manual for Dog's Best Friend*, which promotes adoption of shelter pets and the proper way to treat and train all canines. Signing locations for the new book have included a doggie fashion show and guest appearances by some of the dogs featured in the book.

If you are sending a press release to your alumni magazine or employee newsletter, customize that press release accordingly. Those receiving releases need to be grabbed by its relevance to them.

Book signings and events

Most authors plan on using book signings or events as a major way to publicize and sell their books. Some bookstores enjoy hosting these events; others don't. Some store managers tell us one reason they don't want to host signings is that they don't want an author to feel disappointed if only a few people show up. You cannot count on bookstores to publicize your event. Some will put up, or allow you to put up, a poster in the store or window or announce the event in the store's calendar. But, unless you check, they may forget, or the community relations person, who you think has been so helpful in setting up the program, may leave for the day or quit without making sure that your event is set up.

The first rule of book signings is to hope for sales, but don't be disappointed if you don't make many at a given event. You want publicity, and that is what you are getting. If you have a good product, the store will generally buy a few extra copies to display before and after your visit so that customers who could not attend can buy at another time. Sign the extra copies while you are there so the store can use shelf advertisers for "autographed copies."

Use your printer to create fliers or small posters on colorful bond paper. Use large, easy-to-read type, then put them up on every public bulletin board you can find. Typical locations are supermarkets and Laundromats. Send out your press releases at least two weeks before the event.

> Provide printed shelf-talker hanging cards for the bookstores. Have stickers made for your books that announce: AUTOGRAPHED COPY.
>
> Keep copies of your book in your car. If the store you stop at *doesn't* stock your book, you may be able to make a sale on the spot. This works especially well in an independently owned store, especially in high traffic areas.

In addition to giving copies of the poster to the store to display, see if local motels and time-shares will let you post it on their activity boards. Ask your friends if they can suggest other places that might be good for you to promote your activity.

Print duplicate announcements side by side on copy paper, then cut the sheet in half, and ask the store to give them out to customers or to stuff them in bags at the register the week prior to the signing.

Offer to split the cost of advertising and refreshments with the store. Some large stores may have a marketing department, but don't count on the store to provide your publicity. Many of the superstores have monthly or weekly calendars that they print and distribute to customers and the media. Make sure your information is available to the person making the calendar well in advance of the deadline.

Try to make an "event" out of your book signing. When Dot Bowles was the regional manager for Books-A-Million, she counseled that if you have written a cookbook or gardening book or other how-to-do-it book, have a demonstration. Have music or a history display in conjunction with your book signing to attract customers and interest. Give a short seminar if the subject of your book lends itself to that. Brainstorm with the bookstore manager for ways to build interest in you and your book.

Usually the store will provide a table and chair, but to be sure, ask. If the store has a sound system, ask the manager to announce your signing or event before and during your allotted time, to try to forego general announcements, and perhaps mute or stop store music, during your talk.

The store may not have enough copies in stock for an eye-catching display, so take plenty of copies of your book with you; your table should be stacked full. Write down the number of copies you brought to eliminate confusion when you leave. Typically, the store handles the sales while you do the signing. Find out from the manager on duty if the books are to be paid for before you sign them. If they are, don't sign a book unless the customer first shows you a sales receipt. We have had people come to our programs, pick up a copy of the book, and walk out the door insisting to the check-out clerk that it was a freebie at the program. Not.

Ask each customer how to spell the name of the person to whom the book will be signed. Write the name on a pad, and/or spell it back before making the inscription in the book. You'd be surprised by the variations in the spelling of names, and if you spell it wrong, you have probably wasted a copy of your book. If you goof, save the book to use as a review copy.

 One of our regional TV channels, a network affiliate, had a feature called "Made in Southwest Florida," which appeared once a week on the 6:00 P.M. news. We called the station to ask if books could be considered something made in Southwest Florida because indeed the author, illustrator and the printer fit the demographics. Bingo! A reporter and camera crew were sent to the house, where they filmed the illustrator at work and the author at the computer. We had five minutes of free publicity on television! Heady with success, we talked our way onto the same station's noon news and talk show. The publicity helped us get in area bookstores.

To save time, develop a standard greeting, unless someone asks for special wording.

Talk about your book and your subject whenever you get the opportunity. Visit with customers even if they don't buy your book at the time. The store might make the sale later, and passersby who talk about your book to their friends, might publicize the book through word of mouth.

You may feel a bit like the barker at a carnival, but it's better to talk to people and give them a reason to notice and remember you and your product—the book—rather than just letting them pass by. Stand up and greet your potential customers. You should sit down only to sign books or maybe to take a quick break when no one is in the store. Don't catch up on your reading during the book signing, don't act bored and don't let one or two customers or your friends monopolize your time. Be polite, but keep yourself available for the next customer.

Book signings can be exhausting, and even discouraging sometimes, but they are a good way to keep your name in front of the public, and they do show the stores that you are making every effort to sell the books they have ordered from you.

Do "drive-by" book signings. Drop in at bookstores that have your book in stock just to sign copies or stop at an independent and offer to do a signing on the spot. The store might go for it and you would have a new outlet as well as good public relations. Many readers believe that there is value to autographed copies. By making unannounced visits to bookstores, you may actually stimulate sales and interest in your book. Joan Simonds, owner of the Island Book Nook in Sanibel, Florida, finds that author visits remind her to restock and may stimulate sales while the author is there.

You will find many opportunities to sell your book, but the key is to select those where you have the best opportunity to reach your public. You can take a table at a book or library fair, flea market, or church bazaar, usually quite reasonably. If the fee is high, you might join with other authors to spread the cost. Add in your transportation and other expenses, the cost of handouts, and time away from other projects to see if the exposure is worthwhile. Sometimes it is not. But these affairs offer visibility and give authors an opportunity to network.

If you are having a book sale and signing at a festival, craft fair, or a flea market, or maybe as part of a seminar, make sure you take your own table, chair, books, promotional materials, your receipt book, and a money bag or box with a variety of change. If you will be outdoors you might also want a beach umbrella, a cooler with water or soda, and perhaps a cell phone, and merchant card manual imprinter if you have credit card capability.

Television and radio interviews

Self-publishing authors usually have invested most of their available resources in the production of their book, and often there isn't much money left over for their marketing program. Radio and television advertising campaigns are expensive. Simple television commercials, even if they are produced by a local company, may cost more than one thousand dollars to shoot, and more than one hundred dollars each time they are aired on local network stations. At certain times of the year, local weather channels attract many viewers. Consider contracting for a low-cost trailer to roll across the bottom of the screen to advertise your book or event.

If you really think a commercial will help sell your book, try the local cable channels where air time is usually more affordable. Sometimes packages are available that will lower the cost of each spot if you buy in quantity. But, as with most advertising, you need to show the spot fairly frequently to have it register.

Experts say it usually takes at least three times for viewers to remember or pay attention to what they are seeing or hearing on the tube. Think about your own listening and tune-out habits.

Radio time can also be expensive, although usually less so than television. You may be able to get some free publicity for your book signing by writing up the details for the local radio station or local cable television announcement channel, often called something like "Community Bulletin Board." Radio and TV stations usually need the information ten days to two weeks in advance of the event, so don't wait until the last minute.

If your budget allows, and the subject is appropriate, you may want to take an ad in book trade magazines, book review magazines, or national newspapers or magazines. Be very focused in how you spend your advertising and marketing dollars to get the best results.

Talk shows

The best publicity in life is often free. Get on talk shows. While not free, one way to get the attention of radio and TV talk shows is by advertising in *Radio and Television Interview Report.*

Radio and Television Interview Report, a newsletter sent to station managers and talk show hosts nationwide, consists of quarter-, half-, and full-page display ads that authors and others place to make the industry aware of their books and to express their willingness to be a guest. It is sent to virtually every talk show producer in the country— and it works.

Jo Whatley Cheatham, author of *Homecare: The Best, How to Get It, Give It, and Live with It,* advertised in RTIR and among the calls was an invitation to talk about her book on NBC's "Today Show."

You can also telephone local television and radio stations and talk to the person who books the guests. Give them good reasons why they

 Nature photographer Michael Impellizzeri, author of *Impressions of the Natural World—An Inspirational Journey, Nature's Palette* and *Nature's Artistry,* has used nontraditional methods to sell his books of nature photography and inspirational text. He said, "There are many ways to market books besides the bookstores. These have proven to be successful:

- Targeted my nature photography book to the gift market, especially to nature center gift stores.
- Offered presentations on nature photography with a musical slide show to church groups, civic groups, and private home parties. To gain audience interest, I give one book away as a door prize, and I make my book available for purchase after the program. I have someone collect the money while I autograph the book.
- As a seasonal employee at Yellowstone National Park, I have given a basic photography presentation called "Take better pictures" to employee groups throughout the park. On the promotional flier I tell them that I will give one book away as a door prize and of course, sell books, with someone's assistance, after the program.

"As a result of one of my photo clinics in Yellowstone, a couple wanted to know if I would do the same slide show for their friends when I visited Maryland where I used to live and still have friends. I agreed. Twelve people were invited for dinner. I asked my hosts where to set up the projectors, and to my surprise, they took me to their basement where there were sixty chairs set up. I asked why. It seems that my hosts had invited their church group for dessert and to see my slide show. The presentation had gone on for one and one-half hours when I finally cut it off. The audience response was great. I gave one copy of the book away as a door prize, then announced I would personally autograph my book for those who wanted to purchase a copy. Forty books later I was overwhelmed by the response! Wow! I packed my boxes, thanked my hosts, and left. There have been later sales as a result of that program.

"For the most part, the presentations are offered free with the stipulation that I will have the opportunity to sell my book, but I have also been given an honorarium. By sharing my background and skills with the audience, I have developed my credibility for the book."

should have you on the show. Be bold and creative. Remember, your "audition" is your telephone conversation with them. If you don't seem to have a lively personality and a good phone voice they probably will not invite you to appear on air. Some talk show hosts charge for interviews, so ask up front if there is a fee and if so, what the fees are.

You may not be asked to appear, but perhaps your book will be discussed. Author Kerry Lou had such an experience when Howard Stern talked about her steamy Martian-earthling romance, *Red Planet Blues*: *A tale of interstellar love and the end of the world as we know it.*

Talk show hosts are busy and often have several authors on their shows in a week's time. They may find it impossible to read all the books that are submitted before the interview. To save them and yourself embarrassment:

- Work up a list of questions you would like to be asked and get it, along with a review copy and biographical data and information about you, your book and its topic, to the station well ahead of time. If the interview is to be in person, bring a copy for yourself, too.

- Before your interview, ask if you may mention the 800 number of your fulfillment house or distributor so that callers may immediately order the book. If your host agrees, be sure to mention the number frequently. Sometimes the host will ask you, "Where can people get your book?" as a handy lead-in.

- If you are a guest on a television program, hold up your book now and then for a few moments as you talk so that the cover is visible. Keep the book tipped slightly toward the table so the lights won't be reflected into the camera lens. Better yet, get the host to do it in a way that will insure a close-up.

- Keep your discussion lively and entertaining. Find out in advance what the audience is like so that you can talk to the listeners on their own level.

- Make sure the receptionist at the station has information about how to order your book in case there are calls during or after the show.

- Many radio talk shows can be "patched" (transmitted by phone) right from the comfort of your own home. Joe Sabah suggests that to set the mood, dress as though you were on the show in person, and stand up during the interview as though you were speaking to a live audience. It will do wonders for your presentation.

Best-seller lists

As you are developing your strategy, it's important to be aware that the odds are against making a splash, at least initially, in the national market. Without well-funded marketing and publicity, it is virtually impossible. The *Wall Street Journal*[17] explained how the best-seller lists work. Lists are generated by sales from chain stores, others may take into consideration sales from independents, or drugstore or supermarket distribution.

WSJ staff reporter Patrick M. Reilly noted, "[The] fact is that best-seller lists are . . . subject to the whims of those who compile them, and worst of all, in some cases easy for authors and publishers to manipulate." He added that making the list may determine how the book is promoted in a store or on a shelf. The lists may not include mega-sales through book clubs, or categories of books such as Christian or romance. Making the list is no guarantee that the book is well written or has merit, but only that its marketing program has been successful.

To better your chances of making sales to bookstores and libraries:
- Produce your own promotional book review that you can send to librarians.
- Have a banner made with your publishing company's name or book's title on it that you can display at book signings and book fairs.
- Print bookmarks to include with every book sale.
- Have someone read your book on tape for sale or gifts.
- Get your publishing name in programs, such as theater, sports, or symphony, as a sponsor or advertiser.
- Donate some copies of your book to be given away on talk shows, chamber of commerce open houses or fund-raisers on public television or radio.
- Give a copy of your book to your public radio's reading service to be read on the air to the blind.
- Join with other authors to cooperatively rent and share time at a flea market booth or to host a table at a festival. Split the cost of advertising in catalogs.
- Make your book signings into events.
- Let a good friend plan a special party in your honor (or you plan it yourself) when your book is released. Invitations should be clear that the author will be selling autographed copies of the book and what the price is.

Central New York author Mildred Myers spent a number of years poring through the diaries and letters of Emily Howland, an early advocate of women's rights and a teacher of freed slaves. Miss Howland, who worked closely with other suffragists, such as Susan B. Anthony, had founded a school near Myers' home. The book, *Miss Emily*, is historical fiction—a biographical novel that brings Howland, her lifelong unrequited romance, and her important causes to life. Many years in the writing, the timing of the book's publication could not have been better. The book was released in the summer of 1998, just as the sesquicentennial of women's right to vote was being celebrated in nearby Seneca Falls, New York, and as First Lady Hillary Rodham Clinton was touring historic sites, including the Harriet Tubman Museum in Auburn, New York. Because of Howland's friendship with Tubman, described in *Miss Emily*, the museum presented a copy of Myers' book to the first lady. And the well-written and researched story has had good success.

Myers and her family sold books at the Seneca Falls events, and just about every festival in the region that summer. Myers, who has done historical programs for school children for many years, sometimes appeared in costume as Howland at other gatherings. Her book has been purchased by at least one college for its reading material.

Here's the deal. A Big Guy publisher spends several hundred thousand dollars on media hype when a book comes out, which attracts the interest of the stores. Big splashy ads may attract the attention of trade reviewers who think they will be out of step if they don't comment on the book. The comment may not refer to the book's merits but rather what it is about. That's always a safe approach. Wholesalers and bookstores agree to take an initial order of a sizeable quantity of copies, hoping that the hype will translate into sales. Books are shipped to selected mega-stores. And, *voila!* The new title, because of the number of books *shipped* to the stores from which the best-seller list is compiled, makes the list.

If the book catches on with the public at those stores, it will stay on the list. If not, the copies are returned to the wholesaler, then publisher, before the store must pay for them. It's a bit like the children's game of hot potato. Nobody wants to be caught with the "potato"—lots of copies of books that aren't selling. So books may do a lot of traveling within the sixty- to ninety-day pay periods and quickly end up as remainders or bargain books.

Speakers bureaus

Depending on your subject matter and your public speaking ability, you may be able to promote your book through a speakers bureau. Aside from national celebrities, the bureaus also feature authors on many subjects, such as health, motivation, business, and sports. Many speakers have learned that their audience wants to take something home from the talk.

Mike Frank, author of *For Professional Speakers Only* and founder of Speakers Unlimited, says that it is vital for authors who are considering the speaking circuit to develop a "bureau-friendly" demo tape from ten minutes to an hour in length. Bureau friendly means you should not include references to your address or your telephone number in your video or on your brochure. If you are accepted as a client, all bookings must be made by the bureau and having your personal contact information would create confusion.

 When Heron House Publishers released *Conversations with Mary*, the inspirational story of how the Virgin Mary had appeared to author Barbara Harris at critical points in her life, her husband wanted to do something special to celebrate the book's arrival. The couple planned, along with illustrator Ruth Höök Colby, and her husband, to invite about one hundred friends and members of the press to an afternoon party. The invitations included a copy of the book. At the gathering, Colby's beautiful illustrations were on view, and prints were for sale, as were additional copies of the book. The husbands presented red roses to their wives, and each of them talked about the making of the book, and how Harris's experiences had affected them. The book's debut was a joyous occasion, and Harris received excellent coverage from the reporter who attended.

Also, Frank says, you must indicate your expected fee and other requirements in your cover letter. His book explains how to create the demo tape, and is, itself, an example of how an author has filled a specific niche by putting information in book form, then selling the copies himself at full price.

Nancy Voigl, president of Universal Speakers Bureau told us that "Having a carefully planned, thoughtfully written and quality-produced book is simply smart marketing—as a professional speaker it's the best business card you can have."

Miscellaneous attention-grabbers

When you are presenting a program, or having an autograph session, make use of all the space around you.

- Invest in a sturdy easel and some stiff foam board, then make attractive displays about yourself and your book. Include copies of any reviews or features written about you or your work.
- Have the cover of your book photographed and enlarged to poster size at a photography or discount store, such as a pharmacy, or perhaps your cover designer can provide the image on disk. Get poster frames from a discount store and you will have a dramatic graphic to catch the attention of passersby or for a window display.
- Make magnetic signs for your car. For about fifty dollars, your vehicle will become a billboard for your book, whether you are on the road or parked in town. We have actually sold books to fellow travelers who noticed the magnetic signs at gas stations. Keep your message simple, such as: your name, the book title and either your 800 or home phone number, and Web address. After we recommended the use of magnetic signs to one of our authors, he told us he had sold three books within the first week of using them on his car. Those were only the sales he knew of; there may have been others made at stores.
- Have a friend dress up in a costume relevant to your book (in trade jargon, a "walk-around"). Send your walk-around through the mall with a copy of your book to attract attention and direct people to your signing. Sometimes off-premise (away from the store) advertising by mall stores is not allowed, so be sure to get approval from the mall management first. Obviously some books lend themselves better than others to this approach. And, you can dress up as a character from the book.
- Ask your local bookstore to save extra "dumps" for you, or you can order them from speciality companies. Dumps are the cardboard displays in which large publishing houses often ship their books. They hope that the ready-made displays will get floor or counter

space in the store so their books will be showcased. Bookstores don't have the room for all those displays and throw them away. Pick through what they save for you and keep the ones that fit your book for use at trade shows or book signings. You will have to create your own advertising to paste over what has been preprinted.

- Have your publishing imprint stitched on shirts and caps.
- Have a banner or table drape made with your logo for book fairs and booth displays.
- Create bookmarks printed with information about your book to use as handouts or to leave, with permission, at bookstores and libraries.

Readers' theater and library reviews

A delightful and unusual way to have your book promoted is "readers' theater."

Helen Burns and Lee Buckner of the Books Alive! Readers' Theater Troupe describe the concept: "In readers' theater, you use the author's words with few props, body language and subtle and creative use of your voice the way an artist uses a palette to present scenes of such color and simplicity that the viewer is drawn in from the very first word. Without props, scenery, and stage action, imagination creates the character, the emotion, and the scene. Using the full dramatic possibilities inherent in reading aloud, the performers share the characters' experiences. The tale is further supported and embraced by the readers' inflection and projection, emphasis, and body language."

Librarians do readers' theater; theatrical groups do it, so do colleges and churches. Readers' theater accepts material that is easily adapted to presentation with minimal props and setting. Parts of novels, diaries, plays, newspaper columns, essays, poems, and biographies can be developed into scripts for one or more persons.

During a performance, Burns and Buckner use about five segments from an author's book, and assume different roles simply by changing a hat or other prop, as they act out the selected passages. Buckner said that readers' theater is a tremendous marketing tool. After a performance, audience members always want to locate copies for purchase, and will indignantly call the library if the bookstore is out of copies.

Librarians may also write short book reviews for various editions of a regional newspaper. The reviews feature newly received books of particular interest at county libraries. Reviews are also produced for newsletters of local organizations.

Many library support organizations host fund-raisers, such as book fairs and luncheons, at which local authors are invited to speak and sell their books. We recommend you give a dollar or more per-book-sold back to the organization. You will receive a tax write-off for your donation and will probably be asked back, too.

One of the most extraordinary promotional efforts we have observed was Brofam Books' promotion of *Dino-Man: The Untold Story* by James Brotherton. To sell the action-adventure book involving dinosaurs, aliens, and people from several centuries, this family-owned company had the cover artist create the image of a central character, Ben, an alien. Ben's face first appeared on T-shirts for a local senior league softball team. Every time the team won (and they became state champions), the book's title, *Dino-Man*, was in the sports headlines. That captivated the interest of sports columnists, especially when Brofam challenged the Media All-Stars to a softball game in a stadium as a part of a large community event. (Dino-Man won.) By the time Brofam was ready for its first book signing at Books-A-Million, clerks were wearing the Dino-Man T-shirt, the author came through a smoky, simulated time tunnel in the parking lot, while a local radio station did a live broadcast. Children couldn't wait to touch, hug, and be photographed with the walk-around character of Ben, who had been professionally fashioned by an art studio. Brofam offered free barbecued "Dino-ribs" and cookies, and bookmarks featuring Ben's face. Books sold as long as the family kept up the hype.

Direct mail and bulk mailings

Many self-publishing authors are selling their books successfully by utilizing direct marketing. You can develop your own short list from your holiday card list, friends, relatives, business associates, local clubs and organizations, college friends—anyone you think might order your book or who might tell others about it. For added incentive, offer a prepublication or multiple-copy discount.

After publishing *An Ounce of Preservation: A Guide to the Care of Papers and Photographs,* by Craig A. Tuttle, Rainbow Books did a mailing to genealogical societies and other groups and organizations with an interest in preserving paper. The initial database included 10,000 listings. The direct mailing from the publisher's very focused list resulted in a sales response of between 20 percent and 60 percent. Tuttle also appears regularly on television talk shows and the Discovery Channel's "Home Matters." Rainbow Books has had great success selling books through non-bookstore avenues.

James Kaserman, author of *Gasparilla, Pirate Genius* and *The Legend of Gasparilla: A Tale for All Ages* (Pirate Publishing International), had postcards printed with the cover of his book. He uses the eye-catching postcards to announce the book and his ongoing promotional activities. Kaserman also tags his e-mail messages with information about the book and how to order it. A tireless promoter, Kaserman went on a seventeen-state book tour, selling hundreds of copies. His book was featured in conjunction with Tampa Bay's Gasparilla Festival on the Southwest Airlines' site.

If you anticipate making bulk mailings of fliers and other promotional materials fairly often, you can get a bulk-mail permit from the post office. There is a fee for the permit, and it will need to be renewed every year. If you do not plan to do bulk mailings very often, it is OK to send your mail using another person's permit. Check with local businesses or organizations that have bulk-mail permits. Better yet, find one that has a permit to use "precanceled" stamps. Having a stamp, even a bulk-mail precanceled stamp, on your mailing makes it appear more personal than simply having a preprinted imprint and permit number.

For bulk mail, you must have a minimum of three hundred pieces. All must be the same size and weight, must have exactly the same contents, and they may not include anything handwritten except your signature. With the precanceled stamp program, you are not as rigidly controlled. It is still necessary to have a minimum of three hundred pieces, but within limits, they can vary in size, weight, and content. You still can't have any personal messages except your signature, but it is OK to use computer-generated mail-merge to insert your customers' names, hometowns, and other information, such as the title of the last book they purchased, to make the letter seem more personal. See your local postal service bulk-mail facility for details.

Using the Internet

The Internet is rapidly reaching all parts of the nation and the world, so you may want to consider advertising or communicating through it. Many book distributors, bookstores, authors, publishers, and even publisher's organizations, are advertising or hosting sites on the Web. Some authors report good results from having their books promoted on their Web home pages, others are still waiting for traffic on the information superhighway to come their way. Our general advice is to be aware of the marketing potential of the Web, and try to position yourself to become a part of it, if affordable provider services are available and it suits your needs (see chapter 8).

6 Business details

Getting myself set up to sell my books had an added benefit.
It gave me an unexpected chance to promote my book with people,
such as the clerk at the sales tax office.
—Virginia Testa, author of *The Mystique of God*

There is a lot more to becoming a publishing company—even a *self-publishing* company—than simply deciding that you are going to publish and sell your own book.

Becoming a publisher means becoming a business. Although you should have your basic business plan formulated before you begin, you will need to work on the technical aspects of becoming a publisher while your book is in preparation.

One of the first things you will need to do is select a name and design a letterhead and/or logo. Then, unless you are going to use an ISBN supplied by a packager or another publisher, which we discourage, you will need to apply to R. R. Bowker for a bank of ISBNs as discussed in chapter 4 in the section about credentials. We recommend that you get your own ISBN, because the rights to reprint the book, ampng others, are governed by the ISBN. One of the reasons you are self-publishing is to retain control of your book, and that would include the right to reprint it, even if you retain the copyright. A number of subsidy and vanity presses automatically apply their ISBNs to your book, so this is an area where you need to be savvy.

You will usually have to establish your business formally, that is, register your business or "fictitious" name with the proper agency.

In our area, we needed to register with our county zoning department. To do that, we had stationery made with our company name and address, on which we wrote the cover letter to accompany our application. We were able to create the initial letterhead with our desktop publishing program. Notice of the application was published three times, at our expense, in the legal notices section of one of the local newspapers. When no objections were received, and our type of business reviewed by the zoning department to make sure that we were in compliance with local zoning codes, we were granted an occupational license. In Florida, to prevent the confusion of numerous businesses using the same name, name registry is now handled by the state. Review for zoning compliance is still a local function.

This is also the time to get your business cards and related material

 If you print your e-mail address on your business card, brochure, ads or stationery, *use* it! Read your e-mail regularly and answer it. It is annoying to e-mail someone only to find out that the address is not valid or the person who uses it in an ad never responds to e-mail.

printed. Print in reasonable, rather than large, quantities. Area codes and ZIP codes often change, making printed materials obsolete and useless. To make sure that you do not lose sales or marketing opportunities, we suggest having a dedicated phone line for your fax/modem, and an answering machine. This is also the time to shop around and set up with an Internet service provider and select an e-mail address, if you don't have one. You will want to print your e-mail address on your business cards and letterhead.

Paul Tulenko, who writes a column and has a Web site on small business (www.tulenko.com), recommends that besides taking care of legal details, you should get a mentor, get knowledge (motivational and technical books), get a program (develop a marketing plan), and a business line. He notes that in most communities you can get help from Service Corps of Retired Executives (SCORE) volunteers.[18]

Sales tax

Selling books is the same as selling any other product. Unless you are lucky enough to live in one of the few states that still resists implementing a sales tax, you need to know the rules of, and your responsibilities to, your state Department of Revenue.

In most states, whenever anything (except an exempt item) is sold by a business, sales tax is due. There are certain exceptions, such as when the buyer is another business that plans to resell the product and has a resale certificate (tax number), or when the purchaser is a tax-exempt organization or entity, such as a school or church, or for certain "casual" sales, such as those made at garage sales or items sold by private individuals using classified advertisement. Many new authors are surprised to learn that even the books they give away are subject to sales tax—because tax was not paid on them when they were delivered to the author. Because state tax laws are complex, and vary from state to state, you will need to talk to your local Department of Revenue office for pertinent details.

Keep accurate records of your inventory—where those books removed from inventory went and for what price they sold. Use two- or three-part carbonless sales books and keep the second part for your records. If you are audited by the Department of Revenue you will need this material.

The records of your sales and any personal use of your books will help justify the amount of tax you submit. The amount of tax on each sale is based on the price the buyer pays at the time of purchase, not the list price and not the unit cost, so be sure you note discounts on your sales slips.

If you apply for a sales tax number, let the tax people know when you plan to open your business so that you don't have to fill out tax reports indicating zero sales for several months prior to receiving your shipment of books.

In most states, sales tax is not due when you fill an order from out of state and ship the product to an out-of-state address. Check the rules with your state Department of Revenue or a tax consultant.

Credit card orders

Many self-publishers and small presses function well without being able to take orders with credit cards—especially if they are set up with a fulfillment house with an 800 number that can take credit cards, and pack and ship. However, if you are planning to do your own Internet sales through your Web site, or will be selling your book at trade shows and fairs, you should consider accepting credit card orders.

There are a number of merchant costs associated with credit card sales. Shop around for the best percentage rate you can get. There is quite a difference from bank to bank. You may also be able to save money by purchasing used, rather than new equipment. The fee for reprogramming it for your use is a lot less than purchasing a new merchant card manual imprinter.

If you plan Internet sales, you might want to investigate PayPal, a service that acts as an intermediary to accept credit card sales for you, then passes payment along electronically. Make sure your site is "secure." Buyers are scared off if a warning appears on the screen that the site is not secure. You can make it "secure" by using an encryption program, such as PGP (Pretty Good Privacy) from McAffee.

Keeping records for tax purposes

If you are like many creative types, you might imagine that an ideal world is where there are no checkbooks, bank statements, taxes, or the necessity to keep records or receipts. Your time, you think, is more productively spent writing or painting or thinking. The cold, cruel world of business should not apply to writers, authors, and publishers.

Not true—the more organized you can become before your book is produced, the better. If the process seems overwhelming, find someone to help you—a spouse or a friend, or hire a competent bookkeeper. Taking care of the business details is not as difficult as it may seem, and, thanks to user-friendly computer programs, such as QuickBooks, Quicken or Money, you can keep your records up-to-date easily. If you don't use a computer for bookkeeping, get a *Dome Book* from your local business or office supply store.

Not only will this help you at income tax time, but you will be able to track the number of copies you have sold and at what price. In addition to keeping tabs on production expenses, you can track your advertising and marketing costs, and office expenses including postage, stationery, business cards, Web design and maintenance, or brochures. And at the end of each reporting period you will see how much profit or loss you have from your original investment.

Keep in mind that you will be able to deduct the expenses of your publishing venture from your gross sales on Schedule C of your IRS 1040 form, but you will need accurate and complete record.

And, finally, the IRS expects you to make a profit on your business at least one year out of three or you will not be able to claim business losses against your other income.

The carton mountain

Long before you pace the floor waiting for the delivery of your press run, you must decide where you are going to store your books. If the bulk of the shipment is going to a distributor and/or fulfillment house and the rest to you, make sure your packager or book manufacturer has the shipping addresses and instructions. They will probably add a surcharge for each delivery address you request service to.

If you have ordered only a few cartons for delivery to you for your own use, storage is probably not a problem, but if you are planning to receive a number of boxes, you will want to make arrangements for an air-conditioned storage unit. If you are lucky enough to live in an area with low humidity and can store the books in the garage, keep them off the floor, dry, and away from things that might spill on or run into them.

 Keep a clipboard and pencil handy with your cartons so that you can keep a running tally of the number of boxes you have in stock. Don't open more than one box at a time and make a note of each time you take books out of inventory. That will make it much easier for you to count your inventory at year-end.

 Arrange for your books to be packed in carton quantities you can comfortably lift or handle.

The cost of storage should be figured in the cost of each book so that you can accurately calculate your expenses.

Shrink-wrap

While we're talking about storing your books in a clean, dry place, you might have at least some of your press run shrink-wrapped.

Shrink-wrap is a clear, waterproof, plastic wrap placed around your books before they leave the manufacturer. It shrinks to fit tightly when heated gently and is airtight and moistureproof, and costs about fifteen cents a unit. The advantages of shrink-wrap go beyond storage protection—it may enhance the book's salability. Some buyers like to get books packaged individually, especially coffee-table books. Bookstores will often buy a full package rather than have you break it open for a copy or two. Get an estimate on the cost of shrink-wrapping per book or per package of five or six books.

We recommend asking for a sample of shrink-wrapping from your printer before you order it. Some provide good quality shrink-wrapping, others may substitute the type of wrap that goes around meat in a supermarket.

The disadvantage of shrink-wrapping in several-book packages, aside from the extra cost, is that you will have to break the wrap to get individual copies of your book. To solve that problem, have some cartons packed with loose copies.

Mailing materials and shipping

If you are doing your own mailings, make sure the books are well wrapped so they do not rub against each other, or on the envelope or carton—an advantage of shrink-wrapping. Use padded or stiff envelopes to protect your books from becoming scratched or damaged in transit. We purchase several sizes of sturdy boxes from a carton manufacturer so that we can quickly pack several common order sizes without having to search for a right-sized box or try to jury-rig or pad out an odd-sized empty box from the liquor or grocery store.

We have shipping labels printed with our company name and address to save time in preparing shipments and to give our product a

While *TeleVisionaries,* detailing the history of public television, was being printed, self-publisher Jim Robertson did a direct-mail campaign to public television stations, libraries, and the individuals he had targeted as prospective buyers of his book. The anticipated delivery date was mid-December. To capture holiday sales, Robertson wanted to promise delivery in time for Christmas. He did his homework. He took the measurements and weight of his large, hardbound tome to a pack-and-ship store and purchased several hundred mailing cartons. He addressed labels as orders came in and fastened them to the boxes. When the finished books were delivered (on time, thanks to a special effort by the book manufacturer), Robertson signed and numbered the copies in his limited first edition. He and his wife, Anabel (who had done all her holiday shopping extra early), prepared the books for mailing and took them to the shipping store. Because all the details had been arranged in advance, *TeleVisionaries* was sent out on schedule and the customers received their Christmas presents on time.

professional image. Sadly, even sturdy cartons won't protect your product from uncaring postal clerks. And, when books are damaged in shipping—being bent, dented or getting scratched covers—they will be returned to you, at your expense, by the bookstore, wholesaler or distributor. The proper boxes and packing materials are essential

Get peel-and-stick labels printed that read COMPLIMENTARY COPY, NOT FOR RESALE, or, REVIEW COPY. Put them in an obvious spot on the front cover of your damaged returns, then use them for promotional or review purposes. Obviously you do not want stacks of damaged books, so careful packing for shipping is important, as is the selection of a shipping company.

The U.S. Postal Service's Priority Mail is a convenient, but fairly expensive method of shipping books and other materials. This is ideal for single-copy fulfillment orders. The free, but flimsy, flat-rate cardboard envelope can be stuffed with anything you can fit into it and currently sent for the one-pound rate of $3.85, regardless of zone. If you have several books or something too bulky to fit in the flat-rate envelope and still wish to use Priority Mail, you will need to use a box or sack (also free), which will be charged for based on weight and

If you are not using a distributor or a fulfillment house, consider making arrangements with a neighborhood pack-and-ship store to handle your book shipments.

 Save and recycle packing materials for your own shipping. This includes sturdy cartons, "popcorn," envelopes, cardboard, and plastic bubble pads. Some people buy a paper shredder for the office, then save the shredded paper to use for packing.

If you are sending material to another country, you can use an international express service such as DHL, Airborne, UPS or FedEx, or the somewhat slower, but cheaper, USPS Global Priority Mail.

distance (zone). You can predetermine your postage zones and fees by going to Postal Explorer at http://pe.usps.gov.

In response to concerns about airplane security, the Federal Aviation Administration (FAA) and the U.S. Postal Service have announced that all packages that weigh more than sixteen ounces, being shipped by air in an aircraft carrying passengers (Priority and First-class mail), must be passed *over the counter* at the post office or handed to your carrier. Don't drop them in a drop box, they will likely come right back. Rules are not as stringent, for the package services, such as FedEx, UPS, and Airborne Express, as their consignments travel in aircraft that do not carry passengers.

United Parcel Service (UPS) and Airborne Express have instituted an overnight, all-you-can-pack-into-a-special envelope programs. Airborne's can be obtained prepaid so you just put them in a drop box.

If you are sending a larger order, perhaps to a wholesaler, sending by USPS Media Rate or Bound Printed Matter (a fifteen-pound limit), or by UPS or FedEx Ground is much less expensive, but material sent this way travels by ground transportation only.

Some publishing associations have arranged valuable shipping discounts for their members. The savings in shipping with a carrier such as FedEx Ground or Airborne as a member of SPAN or PMA, for example, may easily pay for the organization's membership fee.

David Dunn, president of Dunn & Company, Inc., in Clinton, Massachusetts, is one of the most resourceful people we've met. He has a book "repair" business that can replace covers and pages after the press run has been delivered and a problem has been discovered. Dunn is also eloquent on how to save money shipping your books. You can contact him for a rate chart (see appendix D), or do some leg work yourself to see how you can save by shipping your book orders by various designations or combinations of classifications, or by United Parcel Service and some of the other alternative delivery services.

7 Riding the distribution roller coaster

*Many publishers feel the benefits received from a distributor are far
outweighed by the costs and loss of control. You don't need a
distributor to get your book into the national market.*
—Dennis Fried, Ph.D., coauthor of *Memoirs of a Papillon:
The Canine Guide to Living with Humans*

OK, you have done your market research homework before getting
your book packaged and you are sure you know who your readers will
be and how you will reach them. The book is in the final stages of
preparation and you expect it to be sent soon for printing and binding.
Now it is time to set up your deals with the bookstores and other retail
outlets so all those eager readers will be able to rush down and plunk
money on the counter.

Down you go to the local mall with galleys in hand, but at one
chain store after another it is the same story: "Where can we order it?"
"Why, you can buy it from me. How many copies can I reserve for
you?" "I'm sorry, but we can't buy from you. Which company is doing your distribution? You must first be on our approved list of wholesalers before we can stock your book."

In order to get your books into most stores, you will have to have
it carried by a distributor or a wholesaler. This chapter will explain
the basics of the distribution system and how it will affect the price of
your book, your potential profit, and the amount of promotional work
you will need to do.

With the ever-increasing volume of new, self-published books on the market, many of them e-published or POD without good editing, it is becoming more and more difficult for first-time authors to reach the retail trade. Many wholesalers and distributors, because of less-than-usual discounts and lack of returnability, decline to carry POD books.

According to Ericka Littles, new title coordinator at Ingram Book Company, Ingram, the largest wholesaler to the retail market, is no longer opening accounts for single-title author/publishers. Ingram is now only ordering those titles through one of its distributor partners. Distributors are also selective in what they carry, and often do not want to deal with single-title authors, especially with those whose books are not professionally produced or without a viable market plan and the money to implement it.

Baker & Taylor will take on single title publishers, but charges an account setup fee. Self-publishing authors and independent presses can still make their titles available through a few other wholesalers at this writing, but the industry continues to change rapidly.

The Barnes & Noble acceptance criteria states that your title must have an ISBN and bar code. It must be available through a wholesaler or distributor, be priced competitively with other titles of a similar topic and quality, and preferably have a perfect binding rather than wire spiral or plastic. You need to send a finished copy, your marketing and promotion plans, trade reviews, and tell how your book is unique in the marketplace. Distributors and wholesalers have similar requirements. No one has room for a book that is poorly produced, not properly credentialed or will not be promoted.

 The distributor you choose can give you important counsel prior to the completion of your book. Work with your packager, designer and distributor on concepts for your title and cover. Consider any tips they give you to make your product more marketable.

 You typically will not be limited in your opportunities to sell to stores other than bookstores. Gift shops, card stores, tourist traps, and specialty stores are a lucrative market and you should work them hard. Promote your product at every appropriate store within a half-day drive. Make follow-up visits every three months.

Distributors

Distributors carry your book on a consignment basis. They usually employ a sales force to call on buyers for the chain bookstores and the larger independents. Distributors also supply the wholesalers with your book. There are national distributors, regional distributors, and even local distributors. Each services a specific area or market. Some specialize in sales to retail outlets, others service public and private libraries, and some sell to educational institutions.

Selling through a distributor will probably return the lowest net profit per copy but it might be the avenue to more sales than any other selling method. A good distribution sales network covers more territory than you can and more personally than the wholesalers can.

Typically an author/publisher will receive 30 percent to 35 percent of the retail price of each book sold. The other 65 percent is divided between the discount to the bookstore (usually 40 percent), the salesperson's commission (5 percent to 10 percent), shipping and overhead, and the distributor's profit. This means if you are planning to sell even *some* of your books through a distributor, you need to set the price at least four times the production cost just to break even; more if you want to cover marketing costs and make a profit. But remember, you need to keep your retail price in line with other books of your genre. That is where you need to work on the size of your press run.

Unless distributor sales are going to be your major sales method, breaking even on these sales is probably not bad. You will make full profit on those books that you sell on your own at cover price, and some profit on those you sell discounted to organizations or markets not covered by your agreement.

Distributors expect an exclusive arrangement with you. In other words, you can't sign on with more than one distributor unless they are noncompetitive. For example, if your distributor does not sell to the library market, you may be able to sign on with a library distributor also. Usually you are not allowed to sell on your own to any bookstores, except maybe to your local independent. The reasoning behind this is: If the distributor's salespeople are to be enticed to work hard to sell your book, they must have the exclusive right to sell. Nothing deflates a salesperson's interest in your book faster than to give his pitch to a buyer, only to find out that the customer has already bought your title from or had it presented by someone else. The distributor's salespeople should be calling on the major independents plus the buyers for the chains and the wholesalers.

Even if you think you have a sizzling topic and the hottest book of the season, the distributor will want to know what your marketing budget and publicity plans are that will help generate sales. That's right, *your* plans! And *your* budget. Don't be surprised if larger distributors expect you to be ready to spend a lot of money to promote your book. The salespeople want to know your marketing plans because their customers, the book buyers, will ask. Your plans, backed by your advertising and marketing dollars, will have a major effect on the sales of the book in their stores. Books that receive national attention often have promotional

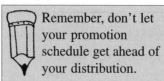 Remember, don't let your promotion schedule get ahead of your distribution.

budgets of several hundred thousand dollars. Publishers count on that kind of money to create the demand for the book. Don't expect the distributor to work in a vacuum.

Distributors print catalogs of their titles with annotations and ordering information in January and July. These catalogs are timed to reach the buyers for the Christmas holiday orders and for the summer reading period. Publishers in the distribution network are often asked to participate by buying a page (or more) to highlight their offerings. These pages vary in cost depending on their placement in the catalog and the number of colors in the print job. Sometimes partial pages are available.

Even though you would like to see your book featured in a catalog, be realistic about its sales potential and do not commit for an ad that will cost more than the profit you will receive from the books sold. If you do not want to buy a display ad, your title will simply be listed in the catalog of titles by subject area. Unfortunately, the salespeople do not spend much time trying to sell from the subject list.

Distributors' catalogs and information about new titles must be available to their sales reps in May. The reps call on their major accounts in June and July, and by August have sold their fall titles. Libraries typically have money to spend after the start of a new fiscal year. So, if your book is not off press until summer or fall, it will be difficult for you to work it through conventional retail distribution channels in time for the holiday season.

Don't waste your money on prepublication hype. If your book is not available to the general public during the promotion, you will have squandered your advertising budget.

Distribution agreements are negotiable. Understand all the costs and requirements of signing up with a distributor beyond the percentage taken. Costs include catalog advertising, storage, shipping orders, and returns. If you are already listed with some stores and other wholesalers, such as those for the library market, you will want to retain your rights to do business with these customers rather than agree to an exclusive arrangement with the distributor.

Most independent publishers think they cannot afford to wait to sell their books until the entire distribution network is arranged. They feel that too much has been invested in the production of the book to sit on the inventory for two to three months. There may be some sales you can generate through mailings, the Internet, direct sales, and fulfillment houses with an 800 number while you hold back on your major publicity blitz.

One advantage to establishing a relationship with a distributor is that often they also serve as a fulfillment center. You may want to work with the latter, however, instead of a distributor.

A fulfillment center accepts orders by mail or through an 800 line twenty-four hours a day, has credit card capability, and ships your book directly to the customer. This means that if you are on a radio talk show in Chicago, you can direct listeners to call the 800 number of your distributor or fulfillment center for immediate service. You can also include the 800 number on all your advertisements, on your magnetic signs, and on your business cards. You capture the impulse buyers because they can make that call immediately, and they can charge the book on their credit card. Publishers will generally realize somewhat more profit with fulfillment sales than they will from sales by the sales force because there is no commission. If your distributor does not fulfill, find a fulfillment house to handle your books.

It is important to coordinate your publicity and marketing efforts with the distributor's shipping schedule so that you are not creating a demand for the book in an area before it is actually available. For instance, if you are planning to be a guest on a talk show in St. Louis, let the distributor know in advance so he can alert his sales force

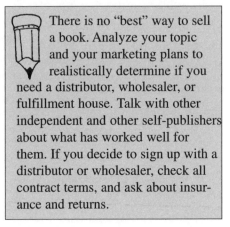

There is no "best" way to sell a book. Analyze your topic and your marketing plans to realistically determine if you need a distributor, wholesaler, or fulfillment house. Talk with other independent and other self-publishers about what has worked well for them. If you decide to sign up with a distributor or wholesaler, check all contract terms, and ask about insurance and returns.

in the listening area. They will then be able to make sure local bookstores have your book to display and sell before, during, and after the show. If you can follow up with personal appearances you will increase your sales.

Distributors usually pay publishers three months after the month the books were sold. Some try to stretch the term longer than that. Do not count on a fast cash flow. Depending on what you owe the distributor for returned books, storage, and advertising, your income from sales may be low or you may even end up with a debt.

Wholesalers

Why do most bookstores purchase only from wholesalers rather than directly from authors or publishers or even distributors? Because it is good business. Wholesalers will stock, or at least make available on order, most titles listed in *Books in Print*. Any number of titles from various publishers can be put on a single invoice and into one shipment, saving time and money for both the shipper and the receiver.

If you want to make your book widely available to bookstores, you *must* have your title available through a wholesaler, such as Ingram

Book Company or Baker & Taylor (see appendix D for a more complete list). Some bookstores only order from wholesalers, so your distributor should try to place your book title with them first. Many wholesalers have a selection process. Ingram has a selection committee that reviews new titles. The process may be waived if the publisher has a large guaranteed order for the book. This book was accepted by Ingram at the same time that Barnes & Noble recommended that *Smart Self-Publishing* be stocked nationwide in all the Barnes & Noble superstores and most of the B. Dalton Bookseller's mall stores.

Chain bookstores have regional buyers who may select a title for regional distribution, depending on its subject.

Typically, wholesalers will ask small publishers for a 55 percent discount, and also will expect them to pay the costs of shipping the books to the wholesale warehouse. The good news is that these usually are not consignment sales. Wholesalers usually *buy* your books to carry in their stock (that is why they have the selection process). The bad news is that you have to wait ninety days for your money, will be required to accept returns (wholesalers also must accept returns from bookstores for damage, overstock or poor sales), and take a charge against money due you. Expect receiving inspectors to be picky about damage and what they will accept.

If your promotion schedule falters or demand dwindles, large numbers of returns can come in *after* you have received (and spent) your money. You will then end up with a debit on your account and will have to return money to the wholesaler or distributor. It can happen to the Big Guys just as well as to unknowns or small presses.

Former speaker of the house Newt Gingrich's science fiction book, *1945*, is an example of a release that did not meet publisher expectations. For every one hundred copies that were distributed, eighty-one were returned, according to an Associated Press story quoting publisher Jim Baen. At the time the story was written, Baen had 97,000 copies of *1945* still in storage.[19]

Even though book wholesalers do not have a sales force out knocking on doors, they may also produce a catalog of their titles. As with distributor catalogs, publishers are invited to buy space. Wholesalers also rely on publisher's hype to create the demand for the book and generate orders.

Small publishers have learned the hard way that the regional offices and warehouses of some national wholesalers operate virtually independently of each other. They do not share inventory information, and do not fill orders received by other warehouses for books that are out of stock at the other warehouse, even though they may be overstocked and about to return the same title to the publisher. If you can, make sure that your book is available at each of the wholesaler's distribution centers, or at least in every one that services an area in which you are going to publicize your book.

If you do not have a distributor yet, or cannot get one to carry your book, try contacting the wholesale companies directly (see appendix D) to find out how you can get your title listed. If you do not anticipate wide readership, ask if the wholesaler has a system for ordering only on request and paying you cash with the order.

Ingram no longer offers its "Ingram Advantage" or "Green Light" programs, which were designed for new publishers. "Self-publishers and small press with fewer than ten titles must now work through one of Ingram's "trading partners" (selected distributors, publishing services or marketing association) to be part of the Ingram system," Ingram's Ericka Littles said.

Like any other aspect of producing or selling your book, you will want to ask for references before you commit to an exclusive arrangement with any distributor or wholesaler and, even then, insist on the right to cancel with reasonable notice. Call some of the publishers the firm represents to determine if they are satisfied with the service.

Some distributors and wholesalers pay according to their contract schedule. Others are notoriously difficult to deal with, leaving small publishers with no payments, a lot of extra charges, confusing accounting systems, and concern that publishers have lost control of their inventory and their investment. Make sure you know all the potential costs, including your marketing effort, from the outset.

PMA distribution program

Publishers Marketing Association (PMA) has a trade distribution program for its members that helps publishers reach the chain stores. Twice a year PMA convenes a committee of representatives from Borders, Waldenbooks, Barnes & Noble, Baker & Taylor, Ingram, Independent Publishers Group, and a few independent bookstore owners. Publishers may submit their book in print to this committee as long as the book has not been previously rejected by the chains or is already under contract with a distributor or sales rep. If the committee accepts the book, the book is presented to the chains for consideration. This sort of program is one way to cut through the barriers that worthwhile books from small press and self-publishers face in reaching the traditional markets. If your book is not accepted, ask why and be prepared to learn from the critique.

Returns happen

Returns are the bane of the publishers, large or small. Here's how returns happen. The publisher creates a retail demand for a book and places the book in the distribution network. The demand creates orders from bookstores (usually through wholesalers or distributors), and the books are shipped. A newcomer to publishing will celebrate. A veteran publisher will know that the marketing must continue to be done to make that book continue to sell, or guess what? The quote "gone today, here tomorrow," attributed to publisher Alfred A. Knopf as he surveyed his warehouse of books, applies to returns. If sales are slack, books will be returned by the bookstore to the wholesaler or distributor, and eventually, to the publisher. The store has really only taken them on consignment, and will want to return them before the bill comes due. If you, the publisher, have already been paid for the copies, you will owe the distributor money when you retake possession of your books. You may also owe a distributor for shipping and storage of the books. And, unfortunately, sometimes the returns are not fit for resale, even on a bargain table. They are scuffed, torn, or even water-damaged.

Tips from Lawrence Webster, public relations person for the Florida Library Association:
- Keep your mailing list updated. Check the Web for lists of state library agencies.
- Join a library friend's group.
- Read a library trade publication regularly.
- Join your state library association and perhaps the American Library Association.
- Subscribe to a library listserv.
- Think about good library homes for your title.
- Visit your library. Sit down and observe how readers select books.
- Read a professional book on library acquisitions and collections development.
- Visit library Web sites, such as ala.org/.
- Take a librarian to lunch. Ask for advice. Listen!
- Make advance appointments and be familiar with, or ask about, policies and learn how decisions are made.

Sometimes the problem is that a hot topic has cooled more quickly than a publisher can sell the books. A competitive book may reach the market first or may be getting all the publicity. Or a chain may model (place a specific number of copies of a title in each store) a book that only sells well in some of the stores.

Michael Taylor, a publishing consultant with years of experience in retail sales, suggests that publishers can reduce their returns by making sure that books are properly produced. That includes making sure the book is well edited. Publishers should know their competition and know that the book has a market. Your book must be as good, or better than, other established books on the market.

Taylor said publishers should be "more selective with the books they publish. Intuition does not work." He suggests using the Internet to do competitive research by looking at Amazon.com's best-seller lists and sales ranking for each title. Also, go to the local bookstore and look at the books that are already on the shelf. "There's no excuse not to spend two or three hours of research on any book you propose to publish. If you want to go ahead and publish the book, you will at least know what you are up against so that you can have realistic expectations."[20]

Libraries use what they call "MUSTY" factors for discarding books when shelves are overcrowded.

M = Misleading, and/or factually inaccurate
U = Ugly, worn, and beyond mending or rebinding
S = Superseded by a new edition or by a better book
T = Trivial, of no discernible literary or scientific merit
Y = Your collection has no use for this material

M is something that can certainly be avoided through careful editing and fact checking.
U can be forestalled by a quality printing job and excellent cover presentation.

Reaching the library market

Like its retail sister, the library market is radically changing. In many areas, acquisition librarians—the people who make the selections for a local library or library system—are being replaced. Libraries are being offered deals by the Big Guys and their distribution sources to take a pre-selected package of titles based in part on what types of books the libraries have ordered in the past. These deals help stretch the budget, but take away the opportunity for local librarians to make their own selections. Of course, there may still be some discretionary dollars, but it may be harder for a one-title self-publisher to reach more than his or her hometown library.

Meanwhile, libraries may still have dollars to spend on old-fashioned selection methods. They make selections based on media reviews, the types of material they need, a book's relationship to the existing collection, special collections or areas of depth, and response to patrons. Be sure to have your family and friends formally request that your book be purchased by their library.

You will still need a library distributor—Baker & Taylor, Quality Books, Unique Books, Brodart Co., Bookhouse Inc., The Booksource, and many others—to help you reach the library market.

There are many types of libraries, not just your local public library. State agencies maintain libraries, as do universities and prisons. There are state archives, legislative libraries, mental health libraries, law libraries and school libraries. States may maintain state-specific collections, i.e., Georgia fiction and Georgia history. Is your book suitable for any of these? You can ask for collection development policies from them.

Libraries expect nonfiction books to have indexes, tables of contents, and all books to have an ISBN, a Library of Congress Control Number, or Cataloging in Publication data, and durability.

Library distributors are full of information that can help you make your book more salable. Like other distributors, their salespeople carry a portfolio of covers and annotations, not books.

Librarians and library distributors have told us that, contrary to popular belief, libraries *are* purchasing softcover books. Softcover editions are less costly, so libraries on limited budgets are able to buy more books. Many books, especially best-sellers and others that may become dated, circulate only a set number of times before they are removed or replaced.

Librarian Helen Burns tells us patrons will often look at a book in the library to "try before they buy." She shares these tips on marketing to libraries and their customers:

- Include ISBN and price on all literature. The easier you make it to buy your book the more apt I am to buy it.
- Include an order form or coupon, but be sure to say *not* to tear it out, but to make a copy. Every week satisfied readers ask me how they can buy a title for themselves.
- If possible, include an 800 number as a service to customers who wish to buy the item. However, library reviewers will not include your personal phone number. That is viewed as advertising.
- Don't promote the book to me and then tell me it is out-of-stock, then send me another flier and another out-of-stock notice.
- Consider your audience. Teenagers love paperbacks, while senior citizens who have arthritic hands thoughtfully evaluate the weight and size of a book.

- Spend time on your title. Test it on family and friends. Do they remember the correct title? Be sure that the title reflects the content of the book.
- If it is a nonfiction book, always have an index.
- If fiction, relate it to another well-known title.
- Name recognition of your company is important and can help sell your books.
- Provide personal information on the author. This makes the books easier to sell to the library public.
- Go where librarians gather and promote to them directly. For example, at a conference arrange for a readers' theater featuring your book. Set up chairs and arrange for refreshments. Share the book and/or presentations with fellow authors.
- Provide bookmarks promoting your title. Librarians always look for new, and inexpensive marketing methods.

The more information librarians have about your book, the more likely they are to recommend it to their patrons. Librarians will hear about your book from the publicity you generate and from the Peter Mars, a retired Boston police officer, uses bookmarks to effectively promote his three books based on true stories—*The Tunnel, A Taste for Money*, and *The Key*. He hands out large bookmarks printed with a picture of each book's cover, a plot summary, and ordering information on the street, at restaurants, in bookstores, and libraries to generate interest and sales.

public's reaction to it. Titles are often purchased as a result of an interview in a newspaper or magazine, a radio talk show, or even a speech to a local club.

Finally, our librarian friends tell us that it's OK to market directly to them. If able, they will purchase books they know their patrons will like right from you, especially if your book isn't available from a distributor's salesperson. It helps if you learn the demographics of the particular library. Librarians work cooperatively with each other and will tell their colleagues about books that are doing well.

The staff at Quality Books emphasizes that while North America's libraries "annually spend billions of dollars for books and videos," it is very hard to reach the individual librarians. Because librarians are faced with selecting from among 60,000 new titles published annually, a full-service library distribution service working by appointment can help sell your book.

The vanishing independent bookstore

An increasing number of the independent bookstores, including some of the really wonderful ones that have been in business for many years, are now being forced to close their doors, overwhelmed by the competition from superstores, Amazon.com, and the major discount outlets. Even the chain bookstores in some major shopping malls are suffering from lost sales due to the heavy discounts offered at nearby Sam's Clubs, Wal-Mart, Kmart, and other superstores. Readers who are looking for bargains rather than a wide selection of titles are attracted to the discount

 Most chains, such as Barnes & Noble, Waldenbooks, Borders, and many independents require titles to be carried by a distributor or wholesaler.
It is tough to get your book accepted by the chains. Many buyers will not return phone calls or acknowledge the receipt of your materials. Be persistent if you think your book belongs in the chains. You will also need to have a distributor or wholesaler for chains to buy from, and for your book to be carried by a distributor, it *must* have an ISBN and bar code.

stores by deeply discounted best-sellers. The impact of the discounts particularly affects independent publishers and self-publishers who, because of higher unit cost resulting from shorter press runs, cannot easily compete with the aggressive discount structure. It is important to learn how your book fits into both the independent bookstores and the superstores.

Many independents are able to buy books directly from an author, but they want to purchase only a quality product, and they want to buy under the same terms that they do with the wholesalers. If you can sell directly to a bookstore, expect to give a discount of 40 percent from the cover price. Often the store will pay at the time of purchase. The larger independents usually buy the same way the chain stores do—only from wholesalers.

Your independent bookstores can still be a tremendous asset if they know and like your book. Joan Simonds, owner of the Island Book Nook in Sanibel, Florida, has "hand-sold" more than 3,000 copies of a single book (*Nathan's Run*), and hand-sells other favorite fiction titles through her personal recommendation. *Nathan's Run* author, John Gilstrap, was so appreciative of her efforts that he sent her an autographed copy of his newest book.

An article by Malcolm Gladwell in the *New Yorker* magazine[21] said that Mary Gay Shipley, owner of That Bookstore in Blytheville, Arkansas, was responsible for "discovering," then personally promoting Rebecca Wells' first book *Little Altars Everywhere*. Wells, now a best-selling author, was unknown when Shipley began telling her patrons to read her. Shipley, like Simonds and other bookstore people who know their books and customers, are trusted advisors and responsible for sales of lesser known books and authors.

They are credible because they are selective. They can't be expected to take on or recommend a book that is poorly edited and poorly constructed, even if you are one of their customers.

A new technology called "collaborative filtering" enables libraries, bookstores (Amazon.com is already using it), magazines, and other companies to hone in very specifically on what customers like based either on past sales or customer questionnaires. New products or books are recommended based on past preferences. The technology works as long as you are ordering for yourself. But if you have been placing gift orders, the recommendations that pop on the computer screen for *you* may not reflect your personal reading tastes at all. Gladwell's article relates the hand-selling by booksellers to collaborative filtering.

Consignment sales to other retail outlets

Often the owners or managers of independent stores will want you to place your book with them on consignment. You should know that consignment sales can be risky. Many things can happen, not the least of which is that you forget where the books are and never go back to check stock or collect your money.

If you do leave your books, be sure you get a signed receipt from someone who has the authority to give it and that you have it in writing that the store will be responsible for the retail price minus the agreed upon discount (usually no more than 25 percent) for each book that is not returned in salable condition. Try to service your consignment accounts once each month, at a time you know the owner or manager will be there to pay you and/or order more books. We do not recommend consignment sales to retail outlets; however, some wholesalers and all distributors will only take books on consignment. If you are dealing with reputable and financially solvent wholesalers or distributors there shouldn't be a problem.

Wanda Jewell, executive director of the Southeast Booksellers Association (SEBA) is emphatic about consignments. "Don't ever put a book on consignment," she said. Instead she suggests working with a commission representative to hype and sell your book.

Commission reps

Publishers Marketing Association says working with a commission rep can be expensive, but is "by far the most effective means of getting books into the book trade. . . . The best reps are very sophisticated players in the book industry. . . . About 60 percent of them belong to a professional organization called the National Association of Independent Publishers Representatives (NAIPR)." PMA suggests you get a copy of the NAIPR pamphlet, "Selling on Commission: Guidelines for Publishers," and the organization's membership directory. SEBA's membership directory also includes the names of a number of commission reps. Jewell suggests contacting the individuals listed for their "rules" (see appendix D for a list of commission reps).

Practically speaking, commission reps are not likely to be interested in a single title from a small press or from a single-title author. They want to show a publisher's line of books, and most self-publishers have just one book. Reps want exclusive rights to sell to accounts in their territories, and expect to be paid a commission on books that someone else, such as yourself, has sold.

Reps carry many lines and are more likely to show new titles from the big houses before getting around to the smaller publishers. It's human nature and where the money is. If you move from self-publishing a book or two to becoming a publishing house producing at least ten titles a year, you may want to consider working with a commission rep who has a relationship with the book buyers at chains.

And, as always, do your homework. Check with other publishers who have been clients of the reps.

Newsstand services

There are many small, regional distributors or jobbers who service newsstands, airports, chain gift shops, or grocery stores. If a location, such as an airport or hotel gift shop, seems like a good one for your title, then find out what company supplies their books and try to get your book accepted. Some of these distributors are easier to "crack" than others. If your book "belongs" at an airport, work at having it placed there. Jack Polidoro, author of *Rapid Descent*, a novel about a plane crash in Boston harbor, managed to have his book placed in several New England airport stores. James Kaserman, author of *Gasparilla: Pirate Genius*, was

 Linda was in the midst of a book signing at a local B. Dalton Booksellers when a man stopped, picked up her books, looked through them, and handed her his business card. He said, "Call my buyer and tell her I said to order your books." It turned out that he ran a distribution service in the Midwest that supplies books to newsstands and bookstores. The service bought two sixty-book cartons of each book—outright. If only all sales were that easy!

able to place his book at the Southwest Florida International Airport. Both books have regional and tourist appeal.

Specialty outlets

Certain books lend themselves best to sales in specialty stores or catalogs—such as cookbooks, books on women's issues, ethnic books, environmental subjects, and gay and lesbian issues. The National Park

Service has gift shops that sell topical history and regional books. Books about animals will find a market at zoos or aquariums.

Some books are a natural fit in gift stores. Most books that appeal to gift store customers are impulse buys—something cute, inspirational or topical well displayed on a counter or with the regional, golfing or cat souvenirs. Or they may be seasonal books.

Because books are primarily purchased on impulse, the title and cover must work overtime to sell the book. Submissions to the gift

An author we know self-published a nicely packaged, well-illustrated children's book that had a Christian—or at least deity—message in it.

A helpful friend took copies of the book to a local Christian bookstore.

The clerk's first question was: "What scripture does it relate to?" The friend tried to explain that the message was one of accepting all people for what they are. But the clerk said the store was not interested unless a specific reference was printed on the cover. If conspicuously printing a scripture reference helps sell the book, then do it!

Because trends change, check with specialty bookstores or distributors to make sure your book has the appropriate information, such as a scripture reference, on the cover, before going to press.

store as well as book store market may be turned down because the title and cover did not suggest who should buy or receive the book.

And, there is a tremendous market for religious and New Age spiritual books in Christian bookstores, and specialty shops.

There are also many niche distributors such as New Leaf, which specializes in New Age and related spiritual topics. Find out the names of regional distributors from bookstores, libraries, other publishers, or publishing associations. You may find one that your book will fit in with. Look for regional distributors that will carry your title or independent jobbers who supply books to bookstores and gift shops in a small area.

We'll say it again. Writing the book may be the easiest part of the project. If a book is not properly produced, it will not make it into the distribution system that serves the bookstore market. Self-publishers must understand the book marketplace in order to break even or make a small profit when books are sold through a distributor at a 65 percent discount from the retail price.

We know authors who have literally walked away from their "baby" expecting it to sell just because it was in a distributor's catalog or carried by a wholesaler. They are usually disappointed and blame everyone else for the book's failure. Authors must help make sales happen either through their own efforts or by paying someone else.

8 Brave new worlds of technology

While e-publishing allows more writers the dream of seeing their words in print, getting their book in the hands of readers is more challenging—and requires rigorous self-promotion. . . . Though new titles stream onto the Web daily, academic and industry observers agree that on-line publishing has a way to go before it takes off.
—Kim Campbell, the *Christian Science Monitor*.[22]

Most people know that virtually as soon as they have purchased a new computer system and set it up, it is obsolete. Technology is changing how we, as author/publishers, and the publishing industry, are doing business at a head-spinning rate. When the first edition of this book was published in 1995, few of us used or even had e-mail. We didn't have personal Web sites and we had not heard of print-on-demand or e-books. Two years later, in the second edition, we provided some basic information about Web sites and added a few e-terms to our glossary. Now, in the third edition we are adding an entire chapter about new technologies.

We are now routinely sending books to book manufacturers on disk rather than as camera-ready, and using print-on-demand technology. In short order, the computer, advanced software programs and the Internet are revolutionizing the way authors, publishers, bookstores, wholesalers, distributors and consumers interact. Keep pace as best you can to take advantage of new opportunities such as selling through the Internet, but don't spend all your marketing dollars or energies on potential Internet sales. There's a lot more to successfully e-publishing or e-selling than posting a book on a Web site.

"The Internet provides a great channel for attracting new customers; penetrating new markets—geographical areas where you don't have 'bricks and mortar;' building the brand; driving to bricks and mortar stores; testing new pricing strategies, promotions, new product lines and improving the customer service experience,"[23] according to Marie Aloisi, a vice president with American Express. She has also noted that while 60 percent of all Internet users regularly shop online, "shopping" often is only window shopping or gathering information, with the purchases still being made at traditional stores.

Bookselling may be an exception. Web bookstore sales—at least for the big sites such as www.bn.com and Amazon.com have been explosive in the past four years, but many Web-based stores have yet to make money. *Publishers Weekly* reported that Web site sales topped $671 million in 1998, a 332 percent increase in sales over the previous year. In 1997, only three-tenths of 1 percent of all books sold were sold via the Internet, according to Michael Hoynes, of the American Booksellers Association. By 1999, the number had increased to 3 percent to 5 percent, and Hoynes predicts that by 2003, the Internet will account for 30 percent of book sales.[24] Even the American Booksellers Association has launched its own Web site, BookSense.com. BookSense carries more than a million titles by allowing small, independent bookstores to sell books on-line—competing as a group against the big independent and chain on-line bookstores.

Web sites are quickly replacing printed catalogs, brochures, and conventional retail stores. Doing business on the Internet saves on telephone calls, postage, and delays in communication. As smart self-publishers, you will need to have your own Web site so you can make the most of the Internet and e-mail. We strongly suggest that to optimize your ability to do business on the Internet, or anywhere else for that matter, you have a second phone line or cable modem installed for your ISP connection, as well as a two- or three-line answering machine with a professional message.

Using the Internet as a publishing tool

The Internet can be a handy tool for authors and publishers. By entering key words in the search engines, you can look up obscure material, check the finer points of grammar, and even have style questions answered on-line. We are book people, so the house, bookshelves, tables, office areas, desks, and available floor space tend to pile up with reference and reading materials when we are working on projects. But a public library we are not. That's where the Internet is useful.

We have researched ballet terms, early American Naval history, spellings of brand names, people, and places. The Internet helps us quickly check facts while we are preparing a book for publication, at least when we are able to find authoritative sites. The key here is the word "authoritative," or you will pick up erroneous information or incorrect spellings from sources that are not credible.

The Internet is also a good place to gather basic information on cover designers, graphic artists, cartoonists, and book manufacturers. But as always, be a good consumer. Once you have explored the Web pages of these service providers, get additional information from them, including a list of references. Ask for samples of their work, and be prepared to return the samples, undamaged, at your own expense after you have looked at them.

You can also use the Internet to do basic market research about your book topic. Go to the sites of on-line bookstores to see what your competition will be. You will be able to quickly determine how many other books on the same general topic are in print and their retail prices—valuable information. You may even find that you have been beaten to the punch. That may initially be disappointing, but knowing there are other books that you will be competing with head-to-head may give you the opportunity to approach the subject in an entirely different way, thereby regaining your market.

You can also visit Web sites of bookstores, groups, or individuals that may have an interest in your topic. When your book is out, you will want to let them know of its availability and how they can order it. Offer to exchange links with their sites.

We know a successful publisher of nonfiction who decided to purchase the rights to a mystery novel. Instead of relying on conventional marketing techniques, Rainbow Books spent several days "working" the Internet, contacting mystery sites and mystery bookstores. The entire first printing was sold shortly after it came off press.

Some new Internet marketing ideas are being tested. For example, members of the Publishers Marketing Association (www.pma.org) can participate in Internet Bookfairs. The PMA site provides members an opportunity to list titles for foreign rights acquisition or remainders.

Your Web site

Many authors and publishers are hoping that, by having a Web site, they will magically sell books. Like everything else, making maximum use of and getting a return on your investment takes work. Don't spend hundreds or thousands of dollars for a Web site design, and then plan to sit back waiting for your book to be "discovered." There are many, many useless Web sites littering the Information Superhighway. Will yours be one of them? Useless means that key words from a site do not register with search engines and that the public can't find it. Or the site may be difficult to read, slow to load or doesn't tell the visitor how to buy your book. If you plan to sell your product on-line, then you should either be able to take credit card orders through your site, or through PayPal, or have a link to a bookstore or fulfillment house that can promptly fill the order. You will also need to have your phone and address listed. Keep your site simple and easy to use. And you will need to register your Web URL with the major and minor search engines and directories.

You will need to promote your site by exchanging links with other sites your potential customers may be visiting. The rules of the road are different for Web marketing than for other types of advertising. For example, most site visitors want instant gratification. They won't wait an inordinate length of time for your home page to load, and they don't want to wade through a long, written text. Your site must be graphically clean, imaginative, and easy to deal with. You will find

Lise LePage's tips about marketing your book on the World Wide Web

Make sure your site is attractive and professional. Your Web site should look as good as your book packaging. Be prepared to spend a little money, either for software and training manuals if you're going to do it yourself, or for outside help to do the things that you're not good at.

Use high-quality graphics appropriate to your topic to reel in site visitors. People will be more likely to read your text if your site is engaging.

Hook your visitors. If your book is a comic novel, make sure your Web site is funny. If you're promoting a nonfiction title, provide some useful or interesting information about your topic. In short, leave your visitors wanting more.

Make it easy for people to buy your book. If Amazon.com stocks it, you can put a free link to Amazon.com on your site. Not only will people be able to instantly buy your book (with no e-commerce set-up on your part) but you will earn a small commission. In addition to Amazon.com, there are many other third-party providers who will collect payment for you in exchange for a commission.

Register a domain for your Web site so that people can get to it easily. Having your own domain costs about $35/year and is well worth it if you want your Web address to be short and easy to remember. Once you've created a Web site, make sure to promote it. List your site with the major search engines. If you do a book signing or talk, mention your URL. Have your URL and e-mail address printed on your business card or other stationery, and don't forget to add it to your e-mail signature.

Stay involved with your Web site. The Web, unlike print, is a forgiving medium. If you think your Web site isn't as effective as it could be, change it.

Above all, have fun! Your potential customers will appreciate the effort and imagination you've expended on their behalf.

Lise LePage is president of MuseArts.com, Inc., a professional Web and multimedia design company based in Brattleboro, Vermont.

that your Web site needs to be somewhat like your back cover—show the book, hype the benefits, give your credentials, and have some testimonials from people who have read it. You can go on from there with links to more pages that have excerpts of the text, and personal information, but don't expect a Web browser to read all about you and your likes and dislikes before they get to the book. They won't and you will lose the sale.

E-stores.com

If your press run quantity and your retail price are balanced properly you should be able to make money per unit, even when discounting to the e-bookstores. We've heard some self-publishing authors complain about the discount schedules mandated by Amazon.com, but our philosophy is that a sale is a sale (and wholesalers take a bigger chunk than e-bookstores). You make less money selling to some outlets, and more to others, but the idea is to reduce your inventory and recapture your investment, and to do it as quickly as possible—before your copyright is so old that you are considered out-of-date.

Most on-line bookstores have programs by which books must be approved, not only for the quality of the subject and writing, but for the professionalism of the book's production, before they are accepted for listing on the site. If accepted, your book is usually posted with a review or annotation. Some allow the publisher, author, or readers to post comments about your book. Some may require that you have an approved wholesaler or distributor.

There are a number of speciality bookstores on the Web and some "real" independent stores also have Web pages. Don't overlook the niche Web stores—travel, mystery, cookbooks, home schooling, Civil War and history, pets, romance—if your book is a fit. Also look into non-bookstore sites for establishing links to your site, or perhaps the operators of those sites will sell your book or have it listed as a

Internet marketing tips from BookZone.com founder, Mary Westheimer

You can improve your standing in search engines by visiting those sites that come up at the top of the results and viewing their page source to see their page titles, page text (the two most important components), metatags and hidden text, then tweak your own. Keep up with the ever-changing requirements of the top directories by reading their individual recommendations and by visiting the Search Engine Watch site at www.searchenginewatch.com.

Reciprocal links can provide 85 percent of a site's traffic. Find appropriate sites through the search engines, using the same words visitors will use to find you. Ask for links (starting with those sites at the top of the engines to piggyback on their visibility!) from these other sites to yours. Save time by simply setting up a link on your end, then asking the other site's Webmaster to follow your lead. Make it easy for them by sending the exact text and code they need.

Find specialty directories by using the search engines. Use your subject search words plus the words "directory," "directories," "indexes," "indices," etc. Each search engine's advanced searching options will be helpful in zeroing in on your best bets.

Your best on-line marketing technique may well be participating in newsgroups and mail lists on your subject, according to a BookZone.com survey of 9,000 publishing-related Web site owners. Those site owners happiest with their traffic participated in these on-line clubs. Don't just post an "ad," though. Take enough time to learn the newsgroup or mail list culture, then post helpful information (see "use a signature" below). To find newsgroups and mail lists in your subject area, visit www.groups.google.com and www.topica.com.

Use a signature (a small text file that is tacked onto the end of your message) in all e-mails. Signatures are especially useful on mail lists, where advertising is frowned upon. By answering questions, conveying news, and exchanging information, you're getting repeat exposures with minimal or no effort and building goodwill. (Your e-mail package should have an option for creating signatures, or you can cut-and-paste a small text file. And do keep it small—Netiquette suggests a signature should be no more than six lines long.)

"Ezines" or "electronic magazines" can keep your name in front of your audiences for minimal cost. A simple sign-up form on your site can build an e-mail mail list in a hurry. Response rates to these on-line newsletters can be phenomenal: 14–22 percent compared to less than 1 percent for ad banners! If your Web host doesn't provide this service, Yahoo does—just go to groups.yahoo.com.

Beat paralysis by dividing and conquering your on-line marketing. Set goals of, say, registering in five search engines each week, establishing four links, and participating in two newsgroups and two mail lists in your subject area. After a month or so, adjust the amounts to your comfort level. For on-line marketing tools, download the free Internet Marketing Toolbox from BookZone Pro at www.bookzonepro.com/mkttoolbox.html.

resource. For example, if you have written a children's book about dolphins and the environment, make sure that the Web sites that cater to home-schooling, wildlife, ecotourism or coastal areas know about your book.

E-books

As people who like to hold a physical book, turn its pages, admire its presence on our bookshelves, and carry it with us to bed or the beach, we are not likely to replace them with electronic books that can be downloaded on-line. But e-books are part of the brave new world of technology and offer a fairly economical way for authors and publishers to have a book "published" without a significant investment.

Many e-book sites offer a print version of the e-book at a reasonable cost. The question is, is it worth an investment $300 to $1,000 per title to have a book available electronically, with single copies printed and bound as ordered? Some entrepreneurs say yes. And, thanks to software such as Adobe Acrobat, eBook Reader, Microsoft Reader and others, books can be stored, downloaded from the Internet and stored in home computers for a price.

Martha Mendoza, a writer for the Associated Press, said that so far the portable e-reader devices have not gained the acceptance or popularity anticipated. Electronic book readers are about the same size as a regular book and can hold as many as ten books or magazines at a time in their memory banks. Pages are turned by simply pushing a button. She said that so far at least a dozen companies had tried to bring the electronic book readers to market, but at this point, none have been best-sellers.

"Publishers have been concerned that electronic versions of their material would be pirated and flood the Internet like illegally distributed music and software, even though the e-books are supposed to be secure," Mendoza said. "Still, publishers have been slow to respond. Only 1,000 titles—mostly older classics—are available for electronic books, well below the 45,000 new titles released in paper last year [1998]."[25]

It didn't take inventive and entrepreneurial folks, such as Stephen King, long to test the e-publishing market. In 2000 he twice experimented with making his writing available on the Internet, asking readers to voluntarily send him $2.50 for his novella *Riding the Bullet* and later, *The Plant*, at $1 per chapter. More than 400,000 people downloaded *Riding the Bullet* in just a few days. His experiments quickly showed that fans were interested only in getting free copies of his book, and also shared them freely with others. Remember, payment was voluntary.

Does that mean that you, as an e-publisher, will be successful in attracting readers? Not likely, unless you have a name as well known as King's and a base of readers who would buy, or at least download, your book. There are many other e-sites rapidly emerging that claim to give publishers and their books exposure. Unfortunately, they seem to be closing just as rapidly. One, Bookface.com, a much-heralded on-line reading company or library, which closed after six months, allowed customers to "open" books on-line and peruse them.

Print-on-demand

It wasn't very long before print publishers such as Lightning Source (a division of Ingram Book Company), CSS Publishing, Sprout, Publisher's Graphics, Mercury Productions, and others took electronic publishing to the next, more useful and viable step, print-on-demand (POD). Packagers, some book manufacturers and several Internet e-publishing sites, such as XLibris and 1stBooks, will accept your book on disk, then print as many or as few copies as you want "on demand" by using new digital technology. The physical quality of the books produced in this manner is good. The samples we have seen appear to be as durable and well produced as many conventional methods of printing. Because POD is only a print method, many books produced this way are not well edited or well formatted.

Many publishers are having their bound galleys printed by POD so that reviewers can see what the cover and book will look like when finished. And for short-run books, reprints of out-of-print books, or keeping alive a book that has reached its life expectancy but still gets a few orders, print-on-demand may well be the answer. It may be ideal for a book that is being tested commercially to see what its acceptance will be before a larger, conventional print run is ordered.

Most of the companies doing POD can print softbound books of various conventional sizes and some are able to produce casebound books. The casebound books usually do not have dust jackets, only foil stamping on the front and/or spine. There is no reason, though, that you couldn't have jackets printed, then apply them yourself. Just be sure you have a proper spine width and allow extra size for the wrap. The specifics are available through your book manufacturer.

POD versus offset printing

Using traditional offset printing (presses, plates, ink, and paper) usually requires minimum press run of 1,000 copies and prepress or "make-ready" charges by the printer—photography, film, plate making, press ready, etc.—that are fairly expensive.

Print-on-demand (POD), on the other hand requires little prepress work, usually the press-ready electronic files are downloaded into the database of the output device and the books are printed directly from those files by machines much like copy machines. The quality of the work, if done by a reputable organization, is as good as offset.

The biggest difference between the two types of printing is cost, and that is good or bad, depending on how you look at it. The initial cost for POD is less than that for offset, but overall, the cost per copy is greater. Both types of printing require the same type of preparation work by the publisher or packager—editorial, typesetting and page design, proofing, cover design, etc., which keeps that part of the cost constant, whichever method you choose. But because POD is a file download, the press expenses are essentially limited to paper and machine time. Individual copies, though, are always the same cost, no matter if you get the minimum 100 or a thousand copies. When you print offset, the unit cost decreases as you print more because the fixed prepress costs are being spread further out among many more copies.

Taking a typical example: A 6 x 9-inch softcover (trade paper-back) book of 224 pages, with a four-color cover, good text stock, and all typesetting, editorial, etc. included, might cost $8,000 for 1,000 copies and $9,500 for 3,000 copies. The same book done POD might cost $5,500 for 300 copies (this includes the prep work) and reprints (minimum of twenty-five copies) might cost about $5 each. The cost per copy will always be $5 (barring material price increases), no matter how many more copies you want. If you run the numbers out, you will find that total cost outlay will even up at about 750 copies POD, and from there on POD will be more expensive.

Publishers usually use offset printing because they are in the business for a profit and, by printing more copies, they can reduce the cost per copy to the point where they can afford to give the 55 percent to 60 percent discount from retail that wholesalers demand. A book that retails for $14.95 will get you $6.73 from a wholesaler and you have to pay the freight to get it there—and the marketing. If that book was part of the above illustration of a 1,000-copy run for $8,000, you would be losing about $2 on every sale. With a 3,000-book run your cost is down to about $3, and you would make about $3 on each book sold. But, you now have to sell 3,000 copies, which may be more than your marketing ability.

Many self-publishers are now opting for POD for two reasons:

1. They can have a small press run of a professionally produced book that will give them the opportunity to test the market. If the books sell well, and they are selling at retail, they can recoup their costs by the 500-copy mark, then either continue to print POD or can switch to offset for a larger press run and lower cost per copy.

2. They have no storage problem because they can keep a stock that will sell easily and can order reprints as needed. Also, if the book does not sell well, there is no pile of books in the garage that needs to be dealt with.

There is another consideration. Because of the unprofessionalism of many POD books (they are often not well edited or properly typeset and do not have professional covers), many wholesalers have discontinued business with new, small publishers. Ingram will no longer open accounts for publishers with fewer than ten titles. Baker & Taylor charges a hefty fee to get an account opened, then only orders when they get an order. They would prefer you deal through a distributor and, because distributors employ sales reps to present books to the store buyers, they demand a discount of up to 70 percent! They will also expect you to invest some of your marketing money in a display ad in their biannual catalogs. This obviously will be a problem for an author with a short run desiring to enter the book trade market.

One POD printer has initiated a "print-and-distribute" program that will provide an automatic listing in a wholesale database, thereby making the book available on a single- or multiple-copy order basis to any bookstore. Publishers are only selected for this program if their books are fully credentialed and professional.

This makes the book orderable on a single (or multiple) copy basis through any bookstore. This means you can use direct mail or other means to announce the publication of your book(s) and say they may be "ordered from the publisher or at any bookstore."

This is a real boost for any small publisher because of the catch-22 nature of the book business—most bookstores can only buy from wholesalers but wholesalers won't take a chance on a new publisher. Payment is made at the rate of about 50 percent of the cover price minus the cost of printing and binding. That $14.95 book would yield a gross profit of $7.48. Subtracting the $5 cost of printing leaves a net profit of $2.48 and the publisher would not have to be concerned with returns or shipping costs.

E-editing and e-quality

Now it is sermon time again. We get preachy about the quality of self-published books because we hate to see good books doomed or discredited for external reasons, such as lack of professional editing, a shoddy cover and lack of credentials. Some of the e-book sites have implied that editing is not important. They have not stressed that a professional cover, design and typography, and editing are important to readers, retail stores and reviewers. This philosophy appeals to writers who either don't know their books need help and/or don't want to pay for professionalism.

These writers proclaim they are "published" and that their book is available. But who wants to read a book riddled with misspellings and lacking in basic punctuation? Just as major print publishers will not be impressed with your book if it is sloppy and requires a lot of work, legitimate e-publishers are concerned about quality issues emerging from vanity Web sites.

Keep in mind, e-book publishing, in general, is nothing more than an electronic printer. A printer prints what he is given, rarely doing professional editing or typesetting.

Present perils of e-publishing and POD

There are other reasons, besides quality, that e-books have yet to gain wide acceptance in the retail market. Judith Appelbaum explained in the PMA newsletter in December 2001[26] that there are economic disincentives for stores to carry them. The POD books cost more per copy, books are nonreturnable and are usually sold at less than the conventional discount schedules. So, while titles may be *ordered* through a store, they are not likely to be stocked, especially by the chains. Quality is uncertain and the PODs are not profitable for the stores.

Digital cameras and publishing

More and more, retailers are extolling the virtues of digital cameras. Understood and used properly, digital photography can be a valuable tool for publishers and authors. All that's necessary is an appropriate camera, image-editing software such as Adobe Photoshop, Photoshop Elements or iPhoto from Apple, and your time and talent. Camera quality is an important consideration as well. In most cases, "you get what you pay for" applies.

Important rules and reminders apply to this new digital medium. Most importantly: "Junk in, junk out." Digital photos suffer from the same problems film photos do, but digital photos can seen immediately, and reshot if necessary, a big advantage of the medium.

Giles Hoover's tips for successfully using a digital camera for your book's images

Digital cameras use an image-size measurement known as "megapixels," which is directly related to how large a photo can be reproduced at the quality necessary for publishing. For instance, for a 6-by-9-inch trade paperback, a cover-size photo should come from at least a 4- or 5-megapixel camera; for interior black-and-white or up to half-page color photos, a 3-megapixel camera should suffice. For larger books consider using traditional photography or smaller digital images.

The photos themselves are commonly JPEG files, the "standard" file format for digital cameras. Be sure to use the "maximum" file-saving setting in order to prevent the loss of quality when the file sizes are made smaller. Once the photos are taken and transferred to your computer, you will need an image-editing program to determine the size and resolution, to make any necessary adjustments, and to convert the image from JPEG format into the TIF or EPS formats appropriate for printing.

Resolution is measured in dots or pixels per inch and commonly referred to as DPI. JPEG photos are usually 72 DPI and need to be reset to 300, the standard for print projects. You should not increase the number of pixels in the photo, just change the resolution. Generally, digital images cannot be made larger without loss of quality.

Photos for book projects can be black and white (grayscale) or CMYK (cyan, magenta, yellow and black, the colors used in four-color printing) color format. RGB (red-green-blue) color, the format monitors and most cameras use, and what your digital photos are most likely stored in, will need to be converted to grayscale or CMYK.

Photoshop Elements, iPhoto, and other basic editing programs offer simple adjustments and grayscale, but not CMYK conversion. Advanced image-editing programs like Adobe Photoshop can make adjustments like cast removal, saturation, and sharpness, and CMYK conversion.

Many experts are available to help with digital photography. Before starting a large project with your digital camera, consider hiring a photographer or graphic designer who advertises digital photo services. A small consultation fee early could save many headaches later on.

Giles Hoover is co-owner of osprey*design, a book design agency in Bradenton, Florida. He designed the cover for this edition of* Smart Self-Publishing *using custom digital photography and Adobe Photoshop.*

Digital photography can bring tremendous flexibility and value to your book project and, with planning, you can add the thousands of words pictures bring. Additionally, after the initial investment in camera and software, there is minimal ongoing cost.

9 Summing things up

*By studying authoritative books on self-publishing, attending
publishers' seminars, networking with other self-publishers,
and learning about the nontraditional markets for books,
the smart self-publisher increases the odds of success.*
—Betsy Lampé, National Association of Independent Publishers

There is much more to creating a book than writing it! Being a smart self-publisher is a combination of being a good consumer, putting your trust in the right people, and understanding and keeping pace with the realities of the world of books.

One way to tap into the many valuable resources available to you is to become a part of a network of self-publishers and small independent presses. Members of these groups have all had the same problems you are now facing, and one of the unique things about publishing is that there is rarely direct competition between publishers. They are happy to answer your questions and share ideas on such issues as marketing and distribution. You may be able to join cooperatively sponsored tables at trade shows or attend informative seminars. Those publishers with books in progress will be able to take advantage of tips and pointers from the experts before their books go to press. Those with books already off press can network about marketing.

Many regions in the country have such organizations for publishers—some are listed in the appendix. We, at Tabby House, are members of Publishers Marketing Association (PMA), Publishers Association of the South (PAS), National Association of Independent Publishers (NAIP), the Southeast Booksellers Association (SEBA), the Florida Publishers Association (FPA), the Small Press Center, and Small Publishers Association of North America (SPAN).

There is much to be gained from each organization. Most have excellent publishing seminars, newsletters, cooperative booths at trade shows, Web sites, and member benefits that can help you save money on shipping and insurance. Some have annual book contests.

Membership in the networking organizations is more diverse than just author/publishers. They also represent vendors—distributors, marketers, agents, book manufacturers, cover designers, and typesetters—who have time to answer individual questions. Attending trade shows and seminars will give you an opportunity to meet and talk with such vendors. The appendix lists many regional associations that you may wish to join.

Seminar speakers, such as John Kremer, author of *1001 Ways to Market Your Book*, or Lloyd J. Jassin, copyright attorney and coauthor with Steven C. Schechter of *The Copyright, Permission and Libel Handbook, A Step-By-Step Guide for Writers, Editors, and Publishers* can give you valuable pointers. Or you may learn about how to submit your book on disk to book manufacturers, about indexing, the library or Internet markets, editing, or trade magazines for independent presses. You may hear a talk about what books are of interest to various public radio shows, or from regional buyers for bookstores. Seminar round-table discussions offer question-and-answer sessions on a wide variety of topics, and often attendees find new outlets for selling their books. That is something we all want to do!

Newsletters from book manufacturers and other vendor organizations are valuable sources of information on many business trends and topics and, if you attend their trade shows, especially as an exhibitor, you will have the opportunity to meet the people who buy books—either by working the crowd or by displaying your book at your own or a sponsored booth.

Trade shows

At the shows you will receive good exposure for your book. And, another benefit—you will make direct contact with many bookstore owners and buyers, and learn firsthand what types of books they are looking for and how they order their stock. Be sure to get their business cards, then follow up shortly after the show with a direct mailing reiterating your special show discount terms or perhaps offering special payment terms, such as a ninety-day billing for holiday orders.

Many publishers have a drawing for a book or other gift to encourage show attendees to leave a card at the booth. As a part of your booth, have your books, promotional literature, and a special trade-show discount posted. You may want to have bookmarks printed that display your book's cover and ordering information. And be ready to write orders. Have order pads, a calculator, discount schedule, and change with you.

One caveat. Many small presses find it frustrating to deal with the independent bookstores, partly because you may need to keep in touch with *each* one to remind the manager to reorder. Many of the independent bookstore owners are disheartened by the growth of the big chains, which can and do offer deep discounts on best-sellers. The buyers for each independent store seem increasingly skittish about ordering from unknown authors or publishers unless the book fits a definite niche and they know they have customers for it.

Attending trade shows and conferences can be an invaluable educational opportunity. You can learn more about the business if you ask questions and listen. You may find yourself in a line with the editor-in-chief of a trade magazine or sitting at a table with booksellers who are talking about how "hot the market is" for preteens because of the Harry Potter series. You can get ideas from other publishers and authors about marketing and displays. You may be able to chat with regional buyers for chain bookstores; owners of independent bookstores; magazine reviewers; representatives from wholesalers, such as Ingram Books; and vendors who offer services that you may later use. Become a part of the publishing/book world, not just a self-promoter.

If you have done your marketing homework and have produced a professional product, you should be able to find a number of appropriate outlets for your book.

You can also purchase mailing lists generated by the trade show organizations and do your own direct mail, targeted at bookstores. Independent bookstore associations may have a list members and their addresses for the price of mailing labels.

Some of the large trade shows, such as that of the American Booksellers Association (ABA), which was sold and renamed BookExpo America (BEA), are costly for small presses. Consider sharing a booth with other publishers and authors to offset the expense and to give you time to roam the floor. Carry a supply of business cards and bookmarks to exchange. Note which stores or buyers are interested in your title and then follow up with a phone call or e-mail.

PMA offers cooperative display and advertising opportunities for members. It also produces an informative monthly newsletter for independent publishers. Executive Director Jan Nathan is refreshingly candid in reporting on the outcome of PMA's participation in various trade shows, such as BEA.

PMA also offers a trade distribution program to help small presses get new titles (that have not already been presented and rejected) into the chains.

PAS has a particularly helpful vendor show concurrent with PAS seminars and SEBA. Vendor members include book manufacturers and printers from the United States and Hong Kong, paper companies and others associated with publishing. You will have a chance to see samples of their work and have your particular questions answered.

And, finally, when working the shows, wear comfortable shoes, as you will need to be on your feet for ten or twelve hours each day. Few books are ever sold while the booth attendant is sitting down.

Be realistic

There are some things that money and industry clout will buy. It is unlikely that you will have your book featured on national television or radio or will see it prominently displayed as a new and notable book in a chain store. The American Booksellers Association and a group of twenty-six independent booksellers filed a suit in federal court in 1998 to force chain stores to give up their discriminatory practices. These practices included offering unpublished discounts not available to the independents and special deals on promotional and advertising expenses. This is what you, as a small press, are up against.

According to author Stacy Mitchell in *The HomeTown Advantage*, it can cost publishers "$750 a month to have a book placed in the 'new and notable' section of a chain store; $3,000 for placing it in the Christmas catalog, $7,500 for store employees to read and promote the book, and $12,000 for the company president's stamp of approval." Independent bookstores might receive significantly less—$50—for displaying a book at the front of the store. These special deals—co-op payments—are out of the financial reach of most self-publishers.[27]

Because of the high cost of ongoing litigation and the likelihood that the judge would rule in favor of the chains, the ABA and their colitigants settled their suit a few days into the 2001 civil trial. There was a monetary settlement that covered some of the ABA's legal costs. The suit brought to light some of the deals the large chains have had with wholesalers that have increased their profits at the expense of others, namely the smaller independent stores.

But that doesn't mean you can't be very successful with your book. Success means sales, passing the break-even point, and making money. Success means establishing credibility as an expert in your field or enjoying having your autobiography or poetry reach a larger audience. Success has as many definitions as there are self-publishers.

Giving up the myths

This brings us full circle in the premise of this book. Smart self-publishing means making a commitment to producing a professional product, developing a marketing strategy, and being willing to promote your book. For most unknown authors, it means giving up these oft-heard notions:

- A self-published author is inferior to one who has yet to be "discovered" by a publishing house.
- Someone else should invest in and sell my book. Authors should not have to get involved in sales.

Betsy Lampé, of Rainbow Books and executive director of the NAIP says, "Self-publishers are 'born' for a variety of reasons. As the large New York publishing houses reduce the number of authors in their 'stables,' those rejected by them continue to seek publication and often turn to producing their work themselves. Other authors become publishers just to maintain control of their work and its production. Some authors just want the lion's share of profits from works they know are marketable. And there are yet others who use self-publishing as a tool to start a publishing house, with an eye toward publishing the works of others."

Times are changing, and even the Big Guys are scouting for successful self-published books to buy for their lines. They are impressed by the entrepreneurial spirit of the self-publishers, especially if they can see proven sales results. You will give your book a better chance to succeed on its own or being picked up by a larger publisher if you do it right. That message is underscored by the following by Christopher Carroll for a Florida Publishers Association newsletter:

As independent publishers, we often feel discriminated against and at a disadvantage when competing with the mega-publishers. Wholesalers and distributors often resist stocking our titles. Bookstores won't buy our books. If they do, they only buy a couple of copies and display them spine out in the wrong section of the store. *Publishers Weekly* won't review our titles. And it's like pulling teeth to get an editor to write a feature story about one of our authors. In short, life is pretty rough for independent publishers.

We could respond to these inequities by giving up. Or by taking the offensive and fighting for what we feel is our due. I would contend that a third option, in the end, will do more to advance our cause. That option is to work within the system that is already in place, instead of expecting the system to flex to meet our needs.

If we want wholesalers and distributors to stock our titles, it is our responsibility to develop books that have obvious value, that includes properly designed covers with the author and title displayed on the spine, and bar codes on the back. We must get the word out to bookstores to create a demand for our books. If we want to sell to bookstores, we need to make the public want to buy our books through promotion. If we want our books reviewed, we need to get review copies or bound galleys to the magazines at least three months in advance of the publication date. And, if we want feature articles written about our books and authors, we need to get the word out to the editors.

In short, if we want the same treatment that the big publishers get, we need to act like professional publishers. Instead of bucking the system, we would do more good for our companies, and for the image of all independent publishers, if we learn to fit into the professional publishing community.

You can be a smart self-publisher

The publishing business can be a grand adventure fulfilling a life dream, or it can be fraught with discouragement and cartons of books stored in the garage. We've tried to provide some basic knowledge of what the marketplace is like, and what you can do to find satisfaction in your project.

- Do your marketing homework. Produce a professional product acceptable to retail and distribution outlets. Be businesslike.
- Be realistic about your press run and the price. If you anticipate retail sales, your price must allow for the standard discounts expected by bookstores and wholesalers.
- If you do not feel confident enough to do it on your own, find and hire a competent, professional, and ethical book packaging company, at least for your first book. Check references.

- Commit yourself to being actively involved in the sale of the book. If you don't do it, who will?
- Finally, network with others in the publishing field and join publishing associations. It doesn't matter if you are networking with one-book publishers or established presses. Pick their brains for ideas, and let them pick yours. There is always something to be learned.

And remember, there is self-publishing and there is *smart* self-publishing. Be one of the smart ones!

Appendix A

The index—last, but not least
Sandi Frank, indexer

What's an index? *Webster's Collegiate Dictionary* defines an index as:

> **in·dex** (in´deks), *n., pl.* **-dex·es, -di·ces**. 1. (in a printed work) an alphabetical listing of names, places, and topics, along with the numbers of the pages on which they are mentioned or discussed. 2. A sequential arrangement of material, esp. in alphabetical or numerical order.

This definition certainly sounds easy and straightforward. In the publishing process, as in the finished book, the index comes last. It cannot be created until pages have been laid out and finalized. By this time everyone, including the author, is tired and worried about the publication deadline. First-time authors who had originally agreed to doing their own index are now faced with the task of actually doing it! Authors often say at the beginning of the process, "How hard can it be to compile an index?" What many authors don't realize is that by the time the proofs of the book are ready, the author is so tired of the material that just the thought of reading it yet again is overwhelming. They usually throw up their hands in despair and turn the project over to a professional—the indexer.

Although the author knows the subject of the book the best, he or she may not be the ideal person to create the index. The author's time is more profitably spent writing. Readers who are just learning about a topic cannot be expected to know everything the author knows. They need an objective guide to the book that a third party [the indexer] can provide. The best possible index will be produced by an indexer, probably in collaboration with the author.

While some publishers have in-house indexers, most indexing is done by freelance people, hired by the author, the publisher, or a book packager. A book packager is an independent business that manages the production of a book by hiring the appropriate people to accomplish the various tasks involved, including copyediting, proofreading, design, manufacturing, and indexing. If the indexer is hired by the publisher, the indexing fee is deducted from the money due the author. If a book packager hires the indexer directly, various payment arrangements can be made.

Authors who wish to index their own books should be encouraged to do so, provided they are made aware of the demands of the task and some of the pros and cons:

- A professional indexer can be objective about the work.
- An author is very close to the work and is therefore unable to envisage how prospective readers will search for information.
- A professional indexer knows how to index a body of work.
- An author knows the subject area but does not usually know how to write an index.
- A professional indexer knows how to budget time so that the publisher or packager receives the index on schedule in the desired format.
- An author usually underestimates the time needed to write an appropriate index.
- A professional indexer is familiar with publishing practices.
- An author is usually among the uninitiated regarding instructions full of publishing jargon.

It is usually a good idea for the author to review an index prepared by a professional indexer. Authors' insights usually result in a better index and a better book.

The place to find a professional indexer is either by referral or by contacting the American Society of Indexers.

Indexers understand that authors know their books best. Whether a professional indexer or the author writes the index, certain general guidelines for a good index should be followed:

- The index should cite narrower topics than the main topics indicate. Broad topics are not useful for the reader when there is a long list of page numbers following a general topic.
- Under no circumstances should an index be an inverted table of contents!
- The choice of good subheadings is what makes a good index.
- The index entries should cite information in the text as concisely as possible. For example, if John Jones is mentioned in the text and J. Jones or just Jones appear in other places, use Jones, John, in the index and cite each page number.
- Cross-references should be used as an aid to the reader, particularly if there is some ambiguity regarding the entry. For example:

  Clemens, Samuel. *See* Twain, Mark
- *See also* references are used when additional information can be found in another entry or subentry. For example:

  Europe, ix, 5-13, 112-130. *See also* individual country names
- If the front matter (introduction, historical notes, etc.) or back matter (appendices) of the book are extensive, then they *should* be indexed. If the front matter merely provides an overview and does not provide substantive detail, then the front matter should *not* be included in the index; if the appendices provide names and addresses, or if there is a glossary, these sections should *not* be included in the index.

As Horace Binney wrote in a letter to S. A. Allibone in 1868, "I certainly think that the best book in the world would owe the most to a good index, and the worst book, if it had but a single good thought in it, might be kept alive by it."

Appendix B

Lessons learned along the way
Dennis Fried, Ph.D.

Ten years ago I completed a humorous memoir about growing up in a small town in the 1950s. I made what I realize now was a very naïve attempt to interest an agent or major publisher and when that led nowhere, I considered self-publishing.

I went to several bookstores and perused their humor sections. All the books there were written by well-known comedians or columnists, and most of these books were not funny. Certainly, I reasoned, there must be many truly humorous books written by non-celebrities—but not one had found its way into the stores. This was valuable information.

If I couldn't get my book into stores, could I sell it through other channels? More fundamentally, who would be my customers? People who like intelligent humor? Aging baby boomers nostalgic for the way it used to be? Not much help from a marketing point of view. Did I believe I could sell lots of books by talking to people at signings, book fairs, etc.? The answer was no. I put the manuscript away.

Three years ago my wife, Katrina, and I had a catered party for our dog's first birthday (my definition of disposable income). I wrote a funny account of the party, as told by little Genevieve, the birthday girl, to send to the guests. Katrina also posted it on the Internet. We got a lot of e-mail asking for more Genevieve stories. After we posted several others, people started asking if the stories were from a book and, if so, where they could buy it.

Genevieve and I got serious. A year later, the manuscript was complete: *Memoirs of a Papillon: The Canine Guide to Living with Humans without Going Mad*, by Genevieve, as told to Dennis Fried, Ph.D. Our back cover barked: "Read This Book Before Your Dog Does! Want to know what your dog really thinks of you? In this hilarious exposé, Genevieve, a two-year-old papillon, takes you into the inner sanctum of dogdom, revealing canine secrets never before shared with humans."

Because I knew I could sell the book myself, and had the money and time (via early retirement from the software industry) to devote to the project, I never considered anything but self-publishing for Genevieve's memoirs. I created Eiffel Press to publish the book, contracted with an established book packager to produce the physical product, and then watched in fascination (horror?) as a tractor-trailer pulled up and disgorged sixty-seven boxes of books into my garage.

That was in the fall of 2000. Since then, the book has become one of the most popular pet titles. It's now [2002] in its fourth printing, for a total of 20,000 copies.

Here are some things I've learned along the way:

- Don't publish a book unless you know very specifically who is likely to pay money for it, and where you are likely to find such people.
- If you self-publish, use a good book packager. It won't cost you much more than acting as your own general contractor, and doing it yourself is likely to lead to defects in the book that will make it unacceptable to stores, and perhaps unappealing to potential purchasers.
- There are no hidden secrets in this business. It's a money game like any other. Before you make any decisions about publishing your book (or having it published), read several books about the industry. My top recommendations are *Smart Self-Publishing*, by Linda and Jim Salisbury; *The Complete Guide to Self-Publishing*, by Tom and Marilyn Ross; and *1001 Ways to Market Your Books*, by John Kremer. If you read such books carefully, there should be no need to pay anyone for consulting.

- Good marketing can sell lots of bad books (and bad movies, bad cars, etc.). Good books with bad marketing won't sell. Marketing is simply making the people who are likely buyers of your book aware of its existence, persuading them that it's a worthwhile purchase—and doing this as inexpensively as possible in relation to the sales income produced.

  Our own marketing strategy has been based on setting up a Web site (www.gvieve.com), maintaining an aggressive signing schedule, getting reviews in dog-related publications, sending press releases to all appropriate venues, scheduling radio and TV interviews (we get them by contacting stations on our own and by advertising in *Radio-TV Interview Report*), and sending hundreds of review copies to bookstores, reviewers, columnists, etc.

- Think very carefully about whether to contract with a distributor (as opposed to wholesalers such as Ingram and Baker & Taylor) and decide only after doing a lot of research. Many publishers feel that the benefits of having a distributor are far outweighed by the costs and loss of control. You don't need a distributor to get your book into the national market. We have no distributor, and our book is in all the bookseller chains nationally, as well as PETsMART. (I'm not saying this was easy!)

- Most of your promotional efforts will generate absolutely nothing (especially ones that cost you money!). I equate my marketing efforts with scattering seeds. Most will not sprout, but a few will, and that's what all the work is for. No matter how good you think your sales letter (or print ad, or news release, etc.) is, if it's not getting some results after a fair trial, change it.

- I debated last year about exhibiting at the Miami International Book Fair, held in November. I doubted whether I could sell enough books to pay for the trip, to say nothing about the hard work and long hours involved. But I've learned that good things often happen on the road, so we went. The *Miami Herald* noticed us (more accurately, noticed little Genevieve, our author-dog) and did a feature story with photo. The story got picked up by the newswires and Paul Harvey talked the book up on his radio show. We got calls from all over the world for radio interviews. Dick Clark talked about the book on his TV talk show "The Other Half." Jay Leno's "Tonight Show" called and requested the book and video samples of TV we've done. (We didn't make the final cut that first time, but Genevieve is a very persistent media hound.)

Of course, most of the time all that happens at book fairs is you get sunburned, or drenched, and sell some books. But the best way to be at the right place at the right time is to be in a lot of wrong ones.

- Big publishers automatically get books into stores (and get many reviewed) because of who they are. You shouldn't resent this. These publishers make billions of dollars each year, mostly through retail channels, and spend millions on placements, co-ops, ads, etc. Of course they have the biggest clout with all the intermediaries between the printing press and the reader. Nevertheless, with a bit of creativity and a lot of hard work, you can get in the game. But to get the distribution channels to open up for you, you first have to *prove* that your book will sell.

How can you do this before your book is in the distribution channels? Several ways, depending on the nature of your book and your own promotional strengths. For example:

> You can arrange signings at independent stores and many chain stores (though you usually must first get your book "approved" by their corporate office). We started building up our résumé with successful signings at area stores, which we then leveraged.

> You can develop a sales history by selling direct via book fairs, lectures, mailings, Internet, etc.

> You can build a portfolio of publicity your book has generated, including radio, TV, print, etc. If you can show that your book creates that type of interest, the distribution channels will get a lot friendlier to you.

- If you're a writer who has published a book, don't be in such a hurry to publish your next one until you've exhausted all reasonable efforts to maximize sales of the first. I've seen far too many cases of writers who are so caught up in their literary self-image that they neglect the rather important business of selling their books.

- Don't get too excited over apparently positive developments, and don't get too crushed by negative ones. No one thing will make your book (possibly not even a national TV appearance), and no one thing will break it.

> *Dennis Fried is publisher at Eiffel Press; see www.gvieve.com. He is reachable at EiffelPress@comcast.net. This article originally appeared in the August 2002* PMA Newsletter *and is reprinted with permission.*

Appendix C

Must-have references

- *Chicago Manual of Style, The*: *The Essential Guide for Writers, Editors and Publishers*. 14th ed., Edited by John Grossman. Chicago: University of Chicago Press, 1993.

- Goldstein, Norm, editor. *The Associated Press Stylebook and Briefing on Media Law*. Cambridge: Perseus Publishing, 2000.

- O'Conner, Patricia T. *Woe is I, The Grammarphobe's Guide to Better English in Plain English*. New York: Riverhead Books, 1996.

- *Merriam-Webster's Collegiate Dictionary*. 10th. ed. Editor in Chief Frederick C. Mish. Springfield, Mass.: G & C. Merriam-Webster, Inc., 1998. Recommended for publishers by *Chicago Manual of Style*.

- Walsh, Bill. *Lapsing Into a Comma: A Curmudgeon's Guide to the Many Things That Can Go Wrong in Print—and How to Avoid Them*. Chicago: Contemporary Books, 2000.

- *Webster's New World College Dictionary*, 4th ed. Editor in Chief Michael Agnes. Cleveland, Ohio: IDG Books Worldwide, Inc., 2001. Recommended for reporters and newspaper editors.

A short list of handy sources

- Appelbaum, Judith. *How to Get Happily Published—A Complete and Candid Guide*. 5th ed. New York: HarperPerennial, 1998. Comprehensive overview of traditional and self-publishing options.

- Appelbaum, Judith and Florence Janovic. *The Writer's Workbook: A Full and Friendly Guide to Boosting Your Book's Sales*. New York: Pushcart Press, 1991.

- Bates, Jefferson. *Writing with Precision*. Washington D.C.: Acropolis Books, 1993.

- Bernstein, Theodore M. *The Careful Writer: A Modern Guide to English Usage*. New York: Atheneum, 1965.

- Bodian, Nat. *The Joy of Publishing*. Fairfield, Iowa: Open Horizons, 1996.

- Borden, Kay. *Bulletproof News Releases*. Marietta, Ga.: Franklin-Serrate Publishers, 1994.

- Bowerman, Peter. *The Well-Fed Writer: Financial Self-Sufficiency as a Freelance Writer in Six Months or Less*. Atlanta, Ga.: Fanove Publishing, 2000.

- Bruder, Mary Newton. *The Grammar Lady: How to Mind Your Grammar in Print and in Person*. New York: Hyperion, 2001.

- Castro, Elizabeth. *HTML for the World Wide Web*. Berkeley, Calif.: Peachpit Press, 1996.

- Crawford, Tad. *Business and Legal Forms for Authors and Self-Publishers*. Allworth, 1990.

- *All-in-One Directory*. New Paltz, N.Y.: Gebbie Press. Lists media sources; available on disk.

- Fadiman, Anne. *Ex Libris: Confessions of a Common Reader*. New York: Farrar, Strauss and Gibson, 1998.

- Gordon, Karen Elizabeth. *The Disheveled Dictionary: A Curious Caper Through Our Sumptuous Lexion*. Boston: Houghton Mifflin Company, 1997.

- Gorden, Karen Elizabeth. *The New Well-Tempered Sentence: A Punctuation Handbook for the Innocent, the Eager, and the Doomed*. Boston: Houghton Mifflin Company, 1993.

- Hacker, Diana. *A Writer's Reference*. Boston: St. Martin's Press, 1989.

- Hirsch, E.D. Jr., Joseph F. Kett and James Trefil. *The Dictionary of Cultural Literacy*. 2nd. ed. New York: Houghton Mifflin, 1993.

- Kirsch, Jonathan. *Handbook of Publishing Law*. Los Angeles: Acrobat Books, 1995.

- Kremer, John. *1001 Ways to Market your Books*. Fairfield, Iowa: Ad-Lib Publications, 1993.

- Jassin, Lloyd J., and Steven C. Schechter. *The Copyright, Permission and Libel Handbook: A step-by-step guide for writers, editors, and publishers*. New York: John Wiley & Sons, Inc., 1998.

- Levin, Martin P. *Be Your Own Literary Agent*. Berkeley, Calif.: Ten Speed Press, 1995.

- *Literary Market Place/The Directory of the American Book Publishing Industry*. New York: R.R. Bowker. Annual comprehensive listing of book publishers, agents, and other resources.

- Merriam-Webster's *Manual for Writers & Editors*: *A clear, authoritative guide to effective writing and publishing*. Springfield, Mass.: Merriam-Webster Inc., 1998.

- Mitchell, Stacy. *The HomeTown Advantage: How to Defend Your Main Street Against Chain Stores . . . and Why It Matters*. Minneapolis, Minn.; Institute for Local Self-Reliance, 2000.

- Neiderst, Jennifer, with Edie Freedman. *Designing for the Web: Getting Started in a New Medium*. Sebastol, Calif.: O'Reilly and Associates, 1996.

- Ortman, Mark. *A Simple Guide to Marketing Your Book: What an Author and Publisher Can Do to Sell More Books*. Bellingham, Wash.: Wise Owl Books, 1998.

- Plotnik, Arthur. *The Elements of Editing: A Modern Guide for Editors and Journalists. New* York: Collier Books, 1982.

- Poynter, Dan and Mindy Bingham. *Is There a Book Inside You? A Step-by-Step Plan for Writing Your Book*. 4th ed. Santa Barbara, Calif.: Para Publishing, 1996.

- Ross, Marilyn and Tom. *Jump Start Your Book's Sales: Revolutionary, Relentless, Result-getting Marketing and Publicity Strategies for Authors and Publishers*. Buena Vista, Colo.: Communication Creativity, 1999.

- Ross, Marilyn and Tom. *The Complete Guide to Self-Publishing*, 3rd. ed. Buena Vista, Colo.: Communication Creativity, 1994.

- Schiffrin, André. *The Business of Books: How International Conglomerates Took Over Publishing and Changed the Way We Read*. London and New York: Verso Books, 2001.

- Short, Carroll Dale. *A Writer's Tool Kit: 12 Proven Ways to Make Your Writing Stronger—Today*. Montgomery, Ala.: Court Street Press, a division of NewSouth, Inc., 2001.

- Strunk, William and E. B. White. *The Elements of Style*. 3rd ed. New York: Macmillan Publishing Co., 1979.

Subscription suggestions

- *Book Marketing & Publicity*
5900 Hollis St., Ste. R2
Emeryville, CA 94608
(800) 959-1059; (510) 596-9300; fax (510) 596-9331
www.infocomgroup.com.
Twenty-four issues per year. Covers marketing techniques and media placement opportunities for small-press publishers, book marketers, and publicists. Comments and suggestions welcomed.

- *Book Marketing Update*
209 S. Main St.
P.O. Box 205
Fairfield, IA 52556-0205
(641) 472-6130; (800) 796-6130
JohnKremer@aol.com   www.bookmarket.com
Published by John Kremer. Marketing information and tips, review and distribution sources, books on publishing.

- *Independent Publisher Online*
400 W. Front St., Ste. 4A
Traverse City, MI 49684-2570
(231) 933-0445; fax (231) 933-0448
www.independentpublisher.com
Reviews and articles.

- *ForeWord* magazine
104 S. Union
Traverse City, MI 49684
(231) 933-3699; fax (231) 933-3899
www.forewordmagazine.com
Bi-monthly news and reviews of books from independent publishers. Timely articles and sections on e-publishing.

- *Publishing Poynters* newsletter
Dan Poynter, publisher, Para Publishing
P.O. Box 8206
Santa Barbara, CA 93118-8206
(805) 968-7277; fax (805) 968-1379
DanPoynter@ParaPublishing.com   www.ParaPublishing.com

- *Small Press Center News*
  Small Press Center for Independent Publishing
  20 West 44th St.
  New York, NY 10026
  (212) 764-7021; fax (212) 354-5365
  membership@smallpress.org   www.smallpress.org
  Membership includes informative newsletter and display of member's
  books at center and opportunity to attend workshops.

Marketing news and tips.

- *PMA Newsletter*
  627 Aviation Way
  Manhattan Beach, CA 90266
  (310) 372-2732; fax (310) 374-3342
  PMAOnline@aol.com   www.pma-online.org
  Excellent compendium of information from the Publishers Marketing
  Association. Good articles.

- *Publisher's Report*
  P.O. Box 430
  Highland City, FL 33846-0430
  (863) 648-4420 (phone/fax)
  NAIP@aol.com   www.Publishersreport.com
  Weekly e-mail newsletter of the National Association of Independent
  Publishers.

- *Publishers Weekly*
  P.O. Box 16178
  North Hollywood, CA 91615-6178
  (818) 487-4500; fax (818) 487-4550
  custserv@espcomp.com   www.Publishersweekly.com
  Know the trends in the publishing industry, includes occasional com-
  mentary about self-publishing. Subscription is increasingly expensive,
  but the information on the book trade is useful.

- *SPAN Connection*
  P.O. Box 1306
  425 Cedar St.
  Buena Vista, CO 81211-1306
  (719) 395-4790; fax (719) 395-8374
  span@SPANnet.org   www.SPANnet.org
  A newsletter published by Tom and Marilyn Ross for members of the
  Small Publishers Association of North America.

Appendix D

Useful stuff for self-publishers

These are names of some people or companies that we have worked with, plus a number we have learned about at trade shows, some from our publishers association meetings, and some from other publishers. The list was up-to-date at the time we went to press, but companies move and area codes change rapidly. *Our list is by no means all inclusive nor is it meant as an endorsement.* We strongly urge that you talk with authors/publishers who have used these services within the last two years for references.

When deciding on your marketing strategies, weigh the cost of your marketing expenses against your desired outcome. Many times the cost of hiring a professional marketing agent will be expensive and will necessitate selling many thousands of books to recoup the cost of the service.

Book manufacturers
- C.J. Krehbiel Co.
  3962 Virginia Ave.
  Cincinnati, OH 45227
  (800) 598-7808; fax (513) 271-6082
  rickh@cjkrehbiel.com   www.cjkrehbiel.com
  Web press (long runs, 10,000 copies or more).

- Central Plains Book Manufacturing
  22234 C Street, Strother Field
  Winfield, KS 67156
  (620) 221-0526; fax (620) 221-4762
  bpate@centralplainsbook.com   www.centralplainsbook.com

- McNaughton & Gunn, Inc.
  960 Woodland Drive
  Saline, MI 48176-0010
  (734) 429-8757; fax (800) 677-2665
  Sheet-fed presses.

- Phoenix Color Corporation
  540 Western Maryland Parkway
  Hagerstown, MD 21740
  (800) 632-4111; (301) 733-0018; fax (301) 791-9560
  www.phoenixcolor.com
  Very versatile, specialty is superior four-color covers and jackets with
  special effects.

- RR Donnelley & Sons Company
  109 Westpark Drive, Ste. 480
  Brentwood, TN 37027-5032
  (615) 371-2113; fax (615) 371-2115
  www.rrd.net
  Sheet-fed and web presses. One of the largest printing houses in the
  world.

- Sheridan Books, Inc.
  100 N. Staebler Road
  Ann Arbor, MI 48103
  (734) 662-3291; fax (734) 475-7337
  mrosen@sheridanbooks.com   www.sheridanbooks.com
  Sheet-fed and web presses. Also does fulfillment and Pick 'n Pack
  shipping. Ask for copy of *Get Ready, Get Set, Go!* Instructions for
  customers on preparing a book for printing and binding.

- Thomson-Shore, Inc.
  7300 W. Joy Road
  Dexter, MI 48130-0305
  (734) 426-3939; fax (734) 426-6216
  www.tshore.com
  Sheet-fed and short-run web press. Publishes free informative
  newsletter. Call to be put on list.

- United Graphics, Inc.
  2916 Marshall Ave. P.O. Box 559
  Mattoon, IL 61938
  (217) 235-7161; fax (217) 234-6274
  www.unitedgraphicsinc.com
  Sheet-fed, short to medium runs.

- Victor Graphics
  1211 Bernard Drive
  Baltimore, MD 21223
  (410) 233-8300; fax (410) 233-8304
  pineapple@victorgraphics.com
  Sheet-fed and web presses. Oversize books and trade paperbacks.

- Walsworth Publishing Co.
  306 N. Kansas Ave.
  Marceline, MO 64658
  (800) 369-2646; (660) 376-3543; fax (660) 258-7798
  www.walsworth.com
  Sheet-fed, small- to-medium press runs, less than 10,000 copies. Good
  work with photos, especially old ones. Does in-house color.

Overseas

- Four Colour Imports, Ltd.
  2843 Brownsboro Road, Ste. 102
  Louisville, KY 40206
  (502) 896-9644; fax (502) 896-9594
  sales@fourcolour.com   www.fourcolour.com
  Good four-color work through either Everbest in Hong Kong or Friesen
  in Canada. Fair prices.

- Regent Publishing
  9327 Rambler Drive
  St. Louis, MO, 63123
  (314) 631-7581; fax (314) 638-5113
  regentstl@aol.com
  U.S. agents for color printers in Hong Kong. Good work.

Short run and Print on Demand

- Central Plains Book Manufacturing
  See listing under book manufacturers.

- CSS Publishing Company (BOD Books on Demand)
  517 S. Main St., P.O. Box 4503
  Lima, OH 45802-4503
  (800) 537-1030; (419) 227-1818; fax (419) 222-4647
  Christian publishers with a BOD department. Good work.

- Lightning Source, Inc.
  1246 Heil Quaker Blvd.
  La Vergne, TN 37086
  (615) 213-5815; fax (615) 213-4426
  www.lightningsource.com

- Mercury Print Productions, Inc.
  50 Holleder Parkway
  Rochester, NY 14615
  (585) 458-7900; fax (585) 458-2896
  mail@mercuryprint.com   www.mercuryprint.com
  Casebound with jacket and soft cover, color and B&W.

- Publishers Graphics, LLC.
  290 Gerzevske Lane
  Carol Stream, IL 60188
  (888) 404-3769; (630) 221-1850; fax (630) 221-1870
  sales@pubgraphics.com   www.pubgraphics.com

- On Demand Publishing
  P. O. Box 720
  Fort Lauderdale, FL 33302
  (954) 761-7282
  www.ondemandpub.com

Bookstore chains

You need publishing credentials plus an arrangement with a wholesaler or distributor to be considered by a chain. Some chains are easier to deal with than others. For a regional topic, begin with a regional buyer.

- Barnes & Noble/B. Dalton Bookseller
  Small Press Department
  122 Fifth Ave.
  New York, NY 10011
  (212) 633-3300; fax (212) 463-5677
  www.barnesandnoble.com

- Books-A-Million
402 Industrial Lane
Birmingham, AL 35211
(205) 942-3737; fax (205) 945-1772

- Borders Group Inc.
Small Press Department
100 Phoenix Drive
Ann Arbor, MI 48108
(734) 477-1100

Book clubs

- Book-of-the-Month Club
1271 Avenue of the Americas
New York, NY 10020-2686
(212) 522-4200
www.bomc.com

- Quality Paperback Book Club
1271 Avenue of the Americas
New York, NY 10020
(212) 522-4200
www.qpb.com

Book repairs

- Dunn & Company, Inc.
David Dunn, president
75 Green St.
Clinton, MA 01510
(978) 368-8505; fax (978) 368-7867
bookdr@booktrauma.com   www.booktrauma.com

Bound galleys

- Graphic Illusions (formerly Crane Duplicating)
9 Martha's Lane
Harwich, MA 02645
(508) 760-1601; fax (508) 760-1544
info@craneduplicating.com   www.craneduplicating.com

- Lightning Source
1246 Heil Quaker Blvd.
LaVergne, TN 37086
(615) 213-5815; fax (615) 213-4426
inquiry@lightningsource.com   www.lightningsource.com

- Royal Palm Press, Inc.
  4288 Jotoma Lane
  Charlotte Harbor, FL 33980
  (800) 214-0023; (941) 627-4800; fax (941) 627-6684
  crane@sunline.net

Contests

- *ForeWord* magazine
  Best fiction and best nonfiction in independent publishing. Judging
  criteria: "Keeping in mind the standards used by booksellers and
  librarians for purchase/acquisitions, judges will take note of editorial
  excellence, intent of book met by author, originality of subject matter,
  accuracy, author credentials, professional packaging and the synergy
  thereof." Prizes. Entrance fee per title. Contact *ForeWord* offices,
  (231) 933-3699 or e-mail karen@forewordmagazine.com

- *Independent Publisher Online*
  400 W. Front St. Ste. 4A,
  Traverse City, MI 49684-2570
  (231) 933-0445; fax (231) 933-0448
  Jim Barnes, editor. Accepts books within year of publication.
  www.bookpublishing.com

- Publishers Marketing Association
  627 Aviation Way
  Manhattan Beach, CA 90266
  (310) 372-2732; fax (310) 374-3342
  info@pma-online.org   www.pma-online.org
  Benjamin Franklin Awards. PMA looks for the "most impressively
  marketed title," excellence in editorial and design, which affect successful marketing programs in a variety of categories.

- Southeast Booksellers Association (SEBA)
  2730 Devine St.
  Columbia, SC 29205
  (803) 252-7755; fax (803) 252-8589
  www.sebaweb.org
  Booksellers vote for favorites in several categories.

- Writer's Digest National Self-Published Book Awards
1507 Dana Ave.
Cincinnati, Ohio 45207
www.writersdigest.com
Entries judged primarily by content and writing quality. Production quality will determine the winner in event of a tie. Entry fee of $100 for first title.

Cover designers

- Abacus Graphics
4701 Morning Canyon Road
Oceanside, CA 92056-4960
(760) 724-7750; fax (760) 724-8788
jrw@abacusgraphics.com   www.abacusgraphics.com

- Dunn & Associates Design
P.O. Box 870
Hayward, WI 54843-0870
(715) 634-4857
info@dunn-design   www.dunn-design.com

- Foster & Foster, Inc.
George Foster
104 South 2nd St.
Fairfield, IA 52556
(800) 472-3953; fax (641) 472-3146
george@fostercovers.com   www.fostercovers.com

- Incite Graphic Design, Inc. (formerly Pearl & Associates)
Chris Pearl
943 S.W. Fifth St.
Boca Raton, FL 33486
(561) 338-0380
pearlart@bellsouth.net   www.pearldesign.com

- Lightbourne
Shannon Bodie
258 A St., #5
Ashland, OR 97520
(800) 697-9833; (541) 488-3060; fax (541) 482-1730
info@lightbourne.com   www.lightbourne.com

- *osprey*design
  Giles Hoover
  600 45th St. W.
  Bradenton, FL 34209-3935
  (941) 746-0144 (phone/fax)
  info@ospreydesign.com   www.ospreydesign.com

- Robert Aulicino Graphic Design
  2031 Holly Drive
  Prescott, AZ 86305
  (928) 708-9445; fax (928) 708-9447
  aulicino@cableone.net   www.aulicinodesign.com
  Cover and text design.

- Robert Howard Graphic Design
  631 Mansfield Drive
  Fort Collins, CO 80525
  (970) 225-0083 (phone/fax)
  rhoward@bookgraphics.com   www.bookgraphics.com

Credentials:

Bar codes

Note: Adhesive bar code labels for already-printed books are available from either Aaron Graphics or Fotel, Inc. Some book manufacturers and most cover designers can generate bar codes.

- Aaron Graphics
  2903 Saturn St., Unit G
  Brea, CA 92821
  (714) 985-1290; (800) 345-8944; fax (714) 985-1295

- Accu Graphix
  3588 E. Enterprise Drive
  Anaheim, CA 92807
  (800) 872-9977; (714) 632-9000; fax (714) 630-6581
  info@bar-code.com   www.bar-code.com

- Fotel, Inc.
  1125 E. St. Charles Road, Ste. 100
  Lombard, IL 60148
  (800) 834-4920; (630) 932-7520; fax (630) 932-7610
  sales@fotel.com   www.fotel.com

ISBN

- R.R. Bowker/ISBN/Advanced Books Information
Diana Fumando, manager
630 Central Ave.
New Providence, NJ 07974
(888) 269-5372
info@bowker.com   www.bowker.com
Title forms for on-line submission.

Library of Congress Control Number

For Preassigned Control Number (PCN):

- Library of Congress Cataloging in Publication Division
101 Independence Ave., S.E.
Washington, D.C. 20540
Note: The Preassigned Card Number Program is now administered
through the LOC Web site: http://pcn.loc.gov/pcn

For Cataloging in Publication:

- Library of Congress Cataloging in Publication Division
Attn: CIP Program
101 Independence Ave., S.E.
Washington, D.C. 20540
(202) 707-9812; fax (202) 707-6345
Library of Congress CIP is not available to self-publishing authors or
small press that publishes books of only one author. Use a PCIP service.
Electronic CIP processing is now encouraged.
Web site: http://cip.loc.gov/cip.

Publishers Cataloging in Publication (PCIP)

- Cassidy Cataloguing Services, Inc.,
111 Frank Rodgers Blvd. S.
Harrison, NJ 07029-1723
info@cassidycat.com   www.cassidycat.com
Specializes in law and business books.

- Quality Books, Inc.
1003 W. Pines Road
Oregon, IL 61061-9680
(800) 323-4241; (815) 732-4450; fax (815) 732-4499
www.quality-books.com

- Unique Books
  5010 Kemper Ave.
  St. Louis, MO 63139
  (800) 533-5446; (314) 776-6695; fax (800) 916-2455

Copyright

- Register of Copyrights
  Library of Congress
  101 Independence Ave., S.E.
  Washington, D.C. 20559

Distributors

- American Wholesale Book Co.
  4350 Bryson Blvd.
  Florence, AL 35630
  (256) 766-3789; fax (256) 764-2511
  Owned by Books-A-Million

- Associated Publishers Group
  1501 County Hospital Road
  Nashville, TN 37218
  (800) 327-5113; (615) 254-2450; fax (615) 254-2456
  www.apgbooks.com

- Biblio Distribution
  Jen Linch
  4720 Boston Way
  Lanham, MD 20706
  (301) 459-3366, Ext. 5507; fax (301) 459-1705
  info@bibliodistribution.com   www.bibliodistribution.com

- Bookazine Co., Inc
  75 Hook Road
  Bayonne NJ 07002
  (800) 221-8112; (201) 339-7777; fax (201) 339-7778
  www.bookazine.com

- Bookmasters Distribution Services
  2541 Ashland Road
  Mansfield, OH 44905
  (800) 537-6727; (419) 589-5100; fax (419) 589-4040
  info@bookmaster.com

- BookWorld Services, Inc.
  1933 Whitfield Park Loop
  Sarasota, FL 34243
  (941) 758-8094; (800) 444-2524; fax (941) 753-9396
  www.bookworld.com

- Consortium Book Sales and Distribution
  1045 Westgate Drive
  St. Paul, MN 55114-9035
  (800) 283-3572; (651) 221-9035; fax (651) 221-0124
  consortium@cbsd
  www.cbsd.com

- Faithworks
  9247 Hunterboro Drive
  Brentwood TN 37027
  (615) 221-6442
  lcarpenter@faithworksonline.com   www.faithworksonline.com

- Independent Publishers Group
  814 N. Franklin St.
  Chicago, IL 60610
  (312) 337-0747; fax (312) 337-5985
  frontdesk@ipgbook.com   www.ipgbook.com

- National Book Network, Inc.
  4720 Boston Way
  Lanham, MD 20706
  (301) 459-3366; (800) 462-6420; fax (301) 459-1705
  www.bibliodistribution.com

- New Leaf Distributing Co.
  401 Thornton Road
  Lithia Springs, GA 30122
  (800) 326-2665 for orders
  (770) 948-7845; fax (770) 944-2313
  www.newleaf-dist.com

- Midpoint Trade Books
  1263 Southwest Blvd.
  Kansas City, KS 66103
  (913) 362-7400
  www.midpointtrade.com
  Sales and distribution for independent publishers. Specializes in New
  Age and spiritual topics.

- Publishers Group West
  1700 Fourth St.
  Berkeley, CA 94710
  (510) 528-1444; (800) 788-3123; fax (510) 528-3444
  info@pgw.com   www.pgw.com

Library distributors

- Baker&Taylor
  2709 Water Ridge Parkway
  Charlotte, NC 28217
  (800) 775-1800; (704) 357-3500
  btinfo@btol.com   www.btol.com

- Blackwell North America, Inc.
  100 University Court
  Blackwood, NJ 08012
  (856) 228-8900; fax (856) 228-6097
  custserv@blacwell.com   www.blackwell.com

- The Book House, Inc.
  208 W. Chicago St.
  Jonesville, MI 49250-0125
  (517) 849-2117; fax (517) 849-4060
  www.thebookhouse.com
  Jobbers serving libraries with any book in print.

- Brodart Co.
  500 Arch St.
  Williamsport, PA 17705
  (800) 233-8467; (570) 326-2461; (570) 326-2461
  bookinfo@brodart.com   www.brodart.com

- Emery-Pratt Company
  1966 W. Main St.
  Owosso, MI 48867
  (989) 723-5291; (800) 248-3887; fax (989) 723-4677
  custserv@emery-pratt.com   www.Emery-Pratt.com
  Orders only when they get an order. No stock.

- Midwest Library Service
  11443 St. Charles Rock Road
  Bridgeton, MO 63044-2789
  (800) 325-8833; (314) 739-3100; fax (314) 739-1326
  mail@midwestls.com   www.midwestls.com

- Quality Books, Inc.
  1003 W. Pines Road
  Oregon, IL 61061-9680
  (800) 323-4241; (815) 732-4450; fax (815) 732-4499
  www.quality-books.com

- Unique Books
  5010 Kemper Ave.
  St. Louis, MO 63139
  (800) 533-5446; (314) 776-669; fax (800) 916-2455

Editors and editing services

Negotiate a per-page or per-project price, rather than hourly rate if possible. Clarify nature of services in advance. Ask for references or samples of work.

- Edit-it
  Chris Roerden, M.A.
  3683 Waterwheel Court
  Greensboro, NC 27409
  1-877-BookEdit; (336) 323-1032; fax (336) 323-1033
  CRoerden@aol.com   www.marketsavvybookediting.com
  Author of *Don't Murder Your Mystery: Self-Edit to Sell* and the forth-coming *Nine Needs of All Nonfiction: Self-Edit to Sell.*

- Elizabeth S. Brent
  esb@umich.edu

- 1stBooks Library Freelance Editor Program
  www.1stbooks.com
  Web site lists screened, freelance editors, specialities and charges.

- Marcia Fairbanks
  2875 GSBN A-203
  Naples, FL 34103
  (239) 643-1432
  marciafair@comcast.net

- Mary Jo Zazueta
  To the Point Solutions
  5828 Joanne Court
  Traverse City, MI 49684
  (231) 943-7736; fax (231) 943-7820
  zazattc@traverse.net
  Also designs interior text and covers.

Fulfillment

- Book Clearing House
  46 Purdy St.
  Harrison, NY 10528
  (800) 431-1579
  www.bch.com
  Fulfillment services and retail distribution for small presses.

- The Intrepid Group, Inc.
  1331 Red Cedar Circle
  Fort Collins, CO 80524
  (970) 493-3793; fax (970) 493-8781
  intrepidgroup.com   www.intrepidgroup.com
  Has free "Publisher's Idea Kit."

- Sheridan Books
  P.O. Box 370
  Chelsea, MI 48118
  (734) 475-9145; fax (734) 475-7337
  www.sheridanbooks.com
  Also a book manufacturer.

Hand-bound hardcovers/bookbinding

- Duvall & Chown
  John Ravenhill
  2267 Main St.
  Fort Myers, FL 33901
  (941) 337-1221

- Olde Towne Bindery
  678 Lake Caroline Drive
  Fredericksburg, VA 22546
  (540) 373-5759

- R&R Bindery Service
  499 Rachel Road, P.O. Box 49
  Girard, IL 62640
  (217) 627-2143

Illustrations/graphic design

- Carol Tornatore Creative Design
  435 Bellini Circle
  Nokomis, FL 34275
  (941) 966-3736
  ctornatore1@comcast.net
  Graphic designer specializing in book design.

- Carrie Kabak
  www.absolutearts.com
  Carriekabak@yahoo.com

- Christopher Grotke
  MuseArts
  41 Cedar St. #1
  Brattleboro, VT 05301
  (802) 254-0129; fax (802) 254-5726
  sites@musearts.com   www.MuseArts.com
  Illustrations, designs, cartoons. Nominated for Caldecott Award. Has
  illustrated several books, including this one.

- Don Doyle
  Eight Damon St.
  North Reading, MA 08164
  (978) 664-6353
  A commercial artist with experience in calligraphy, fine art, and design.

- Joe Kohl
  522 Vine Ave.
  Toms River, NJ 08753
  (732) 349-4149; fax (732) 341-3681
  joekohl@new1.com   www.new1.com/jkohl
  Illustrator for book and magazine publishers and agencies.

- Jon Ward
  2208 River Branch Drive
  Fort Pierce, FL 34981
  (561) 595-0268; fax (561) 595-6246
  hievolved@aol.com
  Illustrator—colorful children's books.

- The Picture Book
  (888) 490-0100
  www.picture-book.com
  A directory of children's illustrators, with portfolios and contact
  information. Published by Watermark, Inc.

- Ralph Smith
  7312 Captain Kidd Ave. #1
  Sarasota, FL 34231
  (941) 924-7963
  ralphsmith11@comcast.net
  Cartoonist with daily strip and does editorial cartoons.

Indexing

- AccuWrite Professionals
  Sherri Linsenbach
  4536 S.W. 14th Ave.
  Cape Coral, FL 33914
  (239) 549-4400; fax (239) 542-0534
  Sherri@AccuwritePro.com   www.writebooks.com

- Hazel Blumberg-McKee
  13418 N. Meridian Road
  Tallahassee, FL 32312
  (850) 395-7824
  hazelcb@spolaris.net

- Hohner WordDesign
  Sharon H. Sweeney, Ph.D.
  515 S. Washington St.
  Smith Center, KS 66967
  ssweeney@ruraltel.net   www.hohnerworddesign.com

- Sandi Frank
  95 Furnace Dock Road
  Croton on Hudson, NY 10520
  (914) 788-3800; fax (914) 271-2095
  sfrankmail@aol.com

Instore book displays

- ABELexpress
  230 East Main St.
  Carnegie, PA 15106
  (800) 542-9001; (412) 279-0672; fax (412) 279-5012
  Floor and counter displays; shipping cartons.

- City Diecutting, Inc.
  2 Babcock Place
  West Orange, NJ 07052
  (973) 736-1224; fax (973) 736-1248
  www.citydie.com

Intellectual property law

- Levine, Sullivan & Koch, L.L.P.
  1050 Seventeenth St. N.W., Ste. 800
  Washington, D.C. 20036
  (202) 508-1100; fax (202) 861-9888

- Libel Defense Resource Center
  80 Eighth Ave., Ste. 200
  New York, NY 10011-5126
  (212) 337-0200
  www.ldrc.com

- Lloyd J. Jassin, attorney-at-law and author
  1560 Broadway, Ste. 600
  New York, NY 10036
  (212) 354-4442
  copylaw@aol.com   www.copylaw.com

- Lloyd Rich, attorney-at-law
  Publishing Law Center
  1163 Vine St.
  Denver, CO 80206
  (303) 388-5215
  info@publaw.com   www.publaw.com

- Reporter's Committee for Freedom of the Press
  1815 N. Fort Myer Drive, Ste. 900
  Arlington, VA 22209
  (800) 336-4243
  www.rcfp.org

Mailing lists

- Library Marketing
  (888) 330-4919
  info@librarymarketing.com   www.librarymarketing.com
  Databases that include the library name, address, phone, fax and e-mail
  addresses. Also includes library's budget for academic and public
  libraries.

- *Mailing Lists that Work: New & Updated Lists*
  Myllymaki & Company
  10 Brooke Circle
  Mill Valley, CA 94941-2203
  (800) 767-1969; fax (415) 381-5056
  Myllco@aol.com

- MCH Mailing Lists
  601 E. Marshall St.
  Sweet Springs, MO 65351
  (800) 776-6373; (660) 335-6373; fax (660) 335-6376
  sales@mailings.com   www.mailings.com

Media resources (national)

- ABC's Good Morning America
  147 Columbus Ave.
  New York, NY 10023
  (212) 456-5900; fax (212) 456-5962
  gma@abc.com   www.abcnews.com

- Associated Press
  50 Rockefeller Plaza
  New York, NY 10020
  (212) 621-1900; (800) 821-4747; fax (212) 621-5469
  pr@ap.org   www.ap.org
  Check Web site for details on where to send specific information.

- Copley News Service
  P.O. Box 120190
  San Diego, CA 92112
  (619) 293-1818; fax (609) 683-7523
  infofax@copleynews.com   www.copleynews.com

- Cox Newspapers
  400 N. Capitol St. N.W., Ste. 750
  Washington, D.C. 20001-1536
  (202) 331-0900; fax (202) 331-1055
  www.coxnews.com

- Gannett News Service
  7950 Jones Branch Drive
  McLean, VA 22107
  (703) 854-6000; fax (703) 558-3813
  www.gannett.com

- National Public Radio
  635 Massachusetts Ave. N.W.
  Washington, D.C. 20001-3753
  NPRLIST@npr.org
  E-mail for list of all NPR program addresses. Write for guidelines for
  submitting ideas for shows such as "All Things Considered."

- The Today Show
  30 Rockefeller Plaza, #304
  New York, NY 10112
  (212) 664-4602

- United Press International
  1510 H St., N.W.
  Washington, D.C. 20005
  (202) 898-8000; fax (202) 898-8057
  tips@upi.com   www.upi.com

Packing materials/shipping supplies

- Uline
  2200 S. Lakeside Drive
  Waukegan, IL 60085
  (800) 295-5510
  www.uline.com
  Call for free catalog.

Publicity/marketing

- CK Marketing
  PMB 305269 Market Place Blvd.
  Cartersville, GA 30121
  infoauthors-speakers.com   www.authors-speakrs.com

- Milton Kahn Associates, Inc., Public Relations
  P.O. Box 50353
  Santa Barbara, CA 93150
  (805) 969-8555; fax (805) 969-2645
  Edgewood9@aol.com   www.miltonkahnpr.com

- Publishing Directions
  50 Lovely St.
  P.O. Box 715
  Avon, CT 06001-0715
  (860) 675-1344; fax (860) 676-0759
  bjauthor@tiac.net

- Publishers Research & Marketing Co.
  1580 Lauderdale Lane
  Bethpage, TN 37022
  (615) 841-3742
  vince.raia@aol.com

- Upper Access
87 Upper Access Road
P. O. Box 475
Hinesburg, VT. 05461
(800) 310-8320
info@upperaccess.com
www.upperaccess.com
Publicity services for publishers and authors. Has free step-by-step publicity guide for book publishers on what to do and when to do it.

Publishers and booksellers associations

These are just a few of the many organizations around the United States. Check the Web sites for BookZone, PMA, SPAN, AAP, and NAIP for links and regional affiliations.

❈ Denotes associations that sponsor trade shows.

- Association of American Publishers, Inc.
71 Fifth Ave.
New York, NY 10003-3004
(212) 255-0200; fax (212) 255-7007
Trade show, newsletters, information.

- Book Publishers of Texas
6387 B Camp Bowie #340
Fort Worth, TX 76116
(817) 247-6016
bookpublishersoftexas@att.net   www.bookpublishersoftexas.com

- Carolina Association of Publishers
c/o "Three Pyramids Publishing"
201 Kenwood Meadows Drive
Raleigh, NC 27603-8314
(919) 773-2080

- Florida Publishers Association
Membership information
P. O. Box 430
Highland City, FL 33846-0430
(863) 647-5951 (phone/fax)
FPABooks@aol.com   www.gate.net/~fpabooks

❈Great Lakes Booksellers Association
P. O. 901
Grand Haven, MI 49417
(800) 745-2460; fax (616) 842-0051
glba@books-glba.org   www.books-glba.org

• Independent Publishers Association of Canada
P. O. Box 1414 Calgary
Alberta T2P 2L6 Canada
(403) 254-0456
www.trickster.com/ipac/

• Independent Publishers of New England
P. O. Box 1164
Northhampton, MA 01061
(413) 586-2388
shel@frugalfun.com

❈Intermountain Independent Booksellers Association
P. O. Box 56
Riverton, UT 21260
(801) 254-1933

• Midatlantic Publishers Association
c/o Bookwise Associates
P.O. Box 50277
Baltimore, MD 21211
(410) 261-5593
info@midatlanticpublishers.org   www.midatlanticpublishers.org

❈Mid-South Independent Booksellers Association
2309 N.W. 120th St.
Oklahoma City, OK 73120
(405) 751-5681; (405) 755-9208
midsouthbooks@juno.com

• Midwest Independent Publishers Association
P. O. Box 581432
Minneapolis, MN 55458-1432
(851) 917-0021
www.mipa.org

❈Mountains & Plains Booksellers Association
19 Old Town Square, Ste. 238
Fort Collins, CO 80524
(800) 752-0249; (970) 484-5856; fax (970) 407-1479
lisa@mountainsplains.org   www.mountainsplains.org

- National Association of Independent Publishers
  P. O. Box 430
  Highland City, FL 33846-0430
  (863) 648-4420 (phone/fax)
  NAIP@aol.com

❋New England Booksellers Association
  1770 Massachusetts Ave., #332
  Cambridge, MA 02140
  (617) 576-3070; (800) 466-8711; fax: (617) 576-3091
  rusty@neba.org   www.neba.org

❋Northern California Independent Booksellers Assoc.
  37 Graham St.
  P. O. Box 29169
  San Francisco, CA 94129
  (415) 561-7686; fax (415) 561-7685
  office@nciba.com   www.nciba.com

- Oklahoma Independent Booksellers Association
  2612 S. Harvard
  Tulsa, OK 74114
  (918) 743-3544; fax (918) 743-5912
  info@stevessundrybooksmags.com

❋Pacific Northwest Booksellers Association
  317 W. Broadway, Ste. 214
  Eugene, OR 97401-2890
  (541) 683-4363; fax (541) 683-3910
  info@pnba.org   www.pnba.org

- Publishers Association of the South
  4412 Fletcher St.
  Panama City, FL 32405
  (850) 914-0766; fax (850) 769-4348
  executive@pubsouth.org   www.pubsouth.org

- Publishers Marketing Association
  627 Aviation Way
  Manhattan Beach, CA 90266
  (310) 372-2732; fax (310) 374-3342
  info@pma-online.org   www.pma-online.org

- San Diego Publishers Alliance
  4070 Goldfinch St., Ste. C
  San Diego, CA 92103
  (858) 794-1597; fax (619) 281-0683
  info@silvercat.com

- Small Press Center
  20 W. 44th St.
  New York, NY 10036
  (212) 764-7021; fax (212) 354-5365
  membership@smallpress.org   www.smallpress.org
  The Small Press Center sponsors an annual book fair, has regular
  readings by small press authors, mounts theme exhibits in its windows
  and bookcases, and offers impressive catalogues of small press books.

- Small Publishers Association of North America (SPAN)
  Marilyn and Tom Ross
  P. O. Box 1306
  Buena Vista, CO 81211-1306
  (719) 395-4790; fax (719) 395-8374
  kate@SPANnet.org   www.SPANnet.org

- South-Central Booksellers Association
  Memphis State University
  1 University Center
  Memphis, TN 38152
  (901) 678-2011; fax (901) 678-2665

✻Southeast Booksellers Association
  2730 Devine St.
  Columbia, SC 29205
  (803) 252-7755; fax (803) 252-8589
  info@sebaweb.org   www.sebaweb.org

- Southern California Booksellers Association
  540 S. Margengo
  Pasadena, CA 91101
  (626) 791-9455
  scba@earthlink.net

✻Upper Midwest Booksellers Association
  3407 W. 44th St.
  Minneapolis, MN 55410
  (612) 926-5868; (800) 784-7522; fax (612) 926-6657
  umbaoffice@aol.com   www.abookaday.com

Publishers' reps/commission reps

- The National Association of Independent Publishers Representatives
  111 East 14th St.
  Zechendorf Towers, Ste. 157
  New York, NY 10003
  (207) 832-7744; fax (207) 832-6073
  naiprtwo@aol.com   www.naipr.org
  Free marketing material and directory of publishers' representatives
  (commission reps). Publisher reps generally are not interested in
  carrying books from one-book publishers or small presses.

Radio and television interviews/media promotions

- Book and Author Alert
  Open Horizons
  1200 S. Main St.
  P. O. Box 205
  Fairfield, IA 52556
  (800) 796-6130; (641) 472-6130
  www.bookmarket.com
  A mailing by John Kremer of selected titles to 1,500 media contacts per
  month.

- Pacesetter Publications
  P. O. Box 101975
  Denver, CO 80250
  (800) 945-2488; fax (303) 733-2626
  jsabah@aol.com   www.joesabah.com

- Planned Television Arts, Ltd.
  David Thalberg, vice president
  301 E. 57th St.
  New York, NY 10022
  (212) 593-5820
  A media placement and book publicity service. Publicists in daily
  contact with producers from major television talk shows.

- *Radio and TV Interview Reports*
  Bradley Communications Corp.
  135 E. Plumstead
  Lansdowne, PA 19050
  (610) 259-1070; (800) 989-1400; fax (610) 284-3704
  A source of ideas for interviewers and producers. Authors tell us that
  ads produce results.

Remainder buyers

- Book Country
  503 Rodi Road
  Pittsburgh, PA 15235
  (412) 242-8818; fax (412) 243-5114

- Camex International, Inc.
  535 Fifth Ave.
  New York, NY 10017
  (212) 808-4669; fax (212) 682-8400

- Fairmount Books, Inc.
  2316 Delaware Ave., Suite 454
  Buffalo, NY 14216-2687
  (905) 475-0988; fax (905) 475-1072
  customerservice@fairmountboooks.com
  www.fairmountbooks.com

- JLM Remainders
  2370 East Little Creek Road
  Norfolk, VA 23518
  (804) 627-4160; fax (804) 587-7421

Review sources

We strongly urge that you look to nontraditional review sources rather than relying on the ones used by the Big Guys. It is hard to compete. Submit your professionally produced book to catalogs that promote your topic. If your topic is a hunting adventure story, seek out magazines and/or catalogs that specialize in outdoor adventure or hunting.

- *ALA Booklist*
  50 E. Huron St.
  Chicago, IL 60611
  (312) 944-6780; fax (312) 337-6787
  Librarians pay attention to ALA reviews.

- *Bas Bleu, Inc.*, Bookseller by Post
  515 Means St., N.W.
  Atlanta, GA 30318
  (404) 577-9462; (407) 571-6626
  www.basbleu.com
  Delightful, well-written catalog with short reviews by readers. Books must be well-produced, hard-to-find, cannot proselytize, usually in category of fiction, travel, humor, children's literature, biography, cooking, gardening.

- BookReviewClub.com,
  Jennie S. Bev, managing editor
  151 Eastmoor Ave. Ste. 309
  Daly City, CA 94015
  jsbev@prodigy.net   www.BookReviewClub.com

- Fearless Reviews
  www.fearlessbooks.com/Reviews.html
  www.fearlessbooks.com/Indies.html
  Posts new reviews that writers consider to be the "best of the independent press." Reviews are linked to listing of independent bookstores
  (the Fearless Independents).

- *ForeWord* magazine
  Alex Moore, review editor
  104 S. Union Ave.
  Traverse City, MI 49684
  (231) 933-3699; fax (231) 933-3899
  reviews@forewordmagazine.com   www.forewordmagazine.com
  Reviews for small and independent press. Send bound galleys four
  months prior to publication date.

- ForeWordreviews.com
  Authors/publishers pay for signed reviews written by professionals.
  Reviews are published on Web site (not in *Foreword* magazine),
  Ingram's iPage and Baker & Taylor's Title Source II, and may be used
  with attribution in other venues.

- *Independent Publisher Online*
  Jim Barnes, review editor
  400 W. Front St.
  Traverse City, MI 49684
  (231) 933-0445; fax (231) 933-0448
  www.bookpublishing.com
  Accepts books within year of publication.

- *Kentucky Monthly* magazine
  P.O. Box 559
  Frankfort, KY 40602-0559
  (888) 329-0053; (502) 227-0053
  www.kentuckymonthly.com
  Prefers books by Kentucky authors or with Kentucky settings, fiction
  and nonfiction, or books of regional interest, such as cooking and travel.

- *Kirkus Reviews*
  770 Broadway
  New York, NY 10003
  (646) 654-4602; fax (646) 654-4706
  kirkkusreview@kirkusreviews.com   www.kirkusreviews.com
  Primarily reviews fiction. Send two galleys. Get updated submission
  guidelines first.

- *Midwest Book Review*
  278 Orchard Drive
  Oregon, WI 53575-1129
  (608) 835-7937
  mwbookrevw@aol.com   www.midwestbookreview.com
  Send finished copy, not galley, to James A. Cox, editor in chief.

- NAPRA Review
  Matthew Gilbert, review editor
  P.O. Box 9
  109 N. Beach Road
  Eastsound, WA 98245
  (360) 376-2702; fax (360) 376-2704
  www.bookwire.com. Click NAPRA
  New Age titles, bound galleys, or finished books within four months of
  publication date.

- The *New York Times* Book Reviews
  229 W. 43rd St.
  New York, NY 10036
  (212) 556-1234

- NonfictionReviews.com
  David Bloomberg, editor
  david.bloomberg@pobox.com   www.NonfictionReviews.com

- *Publishers Weekly* "Forecasts"
  Jonathan Bing
  249 W. 17th St.
  New York, NY 10011
  (212) 645-9700; fax (212) 463-6631
  www.publishersweekly.reviewsnews
  Submit bound galleys at least three months before publication date.

- *USA Today* Book Reviews
  7950 Jones Branch Drive
  McLean, VA 22108
  (703) 854-3400

Speakers' organizations

- AMU Speakers Bureau
  4520 Main St.
  Kansas City MO 64111-7701
  (800) 255-6734; (816) 932-6600
  speakersbureau@amuniversal.com
  www.amuniversal.com/ups/speakers/

- National Speakers Association
  1500 S. Priest Drive
  Tempe, AZ 85281
  (602) 968-2552; fax (602) 968-0911
  information@NSAspeakers.org   www.nsaspeakers.org

- Speakers Unlimited
  Mike Frank, CSP, CPAE
  Box 27225
  Columbus, OH 43227
  (614) 864-3703; fax (614) 864-3876
  ProSpeak@aolcom   www.speakersunlimited.com
  Publisher of *For Professional Speakers Only,* for authors who want to work with speakers bureaus. Available through Mike Frank. $24.95.

- Universal Speakers Bureau
  (800) 644-4144; (231) 933-1176; fax (231) 933-6282
  nancyvogl@universalspeakers.com   www.universalspeakers.com

- Washington Speakers Bureau
  1663 Prince St.
  Alexandria, VA 22314
  (703) 684-0555; fax (703) 684-9132
  infor@washingtonspeakers.com   www.washingtonspeakers.com

Specialty printer for video boxes, CD wallets, labels

- Tu-Vets Corporation
  5635 E. Beverly Blvd.
  Los Angeles, CA 90022
  (800) 894-8977; fax (323) 724-1896
  tuvets@aol.com   www.tu-vets.com

Trade distribution assistance

- Publishers Marketing Association
  627 Aviation Way
  Manhattan Beach, CA 90266
  (310) 372-2732; fax 310-374-3342
  www.PMAonline.org
  Offers a trade distribution program twice a year to members by convening a committee of representatives from major chains, and a few independent bookstores. The committee reviews all entered titles and either accepts or rejects the offered title. If you are rejected, you will receive a brief comment as to why. Stipulations: You cannot currently have a contractual agreement with a distributer, you cannot have been rejected previously for the submitted book, and you must be in print.

Typesetting

- Crane Composition
  4288 Jotoma Lane
  Charlotte Harbor, FL 33980
  (941) 627-4800

- Folio Bookworks
  3241 Columbus Ave. S.
  Minneapolis, MN 55407-2030
  (612) 827-2552; fax (612) 827-4417
  info@folio-bookworks.com   www.folio-bookworks.com

- Graphic Composition, Inc.
  240 Hawthorne Ave.
  Athens, GA 30606
  (800) 421-6722; (706) 546-8688; fax (706) 543-9655
  www.gcitype.com

- Huron Valley Graphics, Inc.
  4597 Platt Road
  Ann Arbor, MI 48108
  (800) 362-9655; (734) 477-0448; fax (734) 477-0393
  custserve.hvg.com   www.hvg.com

- To the Point Solutions
  Mary Jo Zazueta
  5828 Joanne Court
  Traverse City, MI 49684
  (213) 943-7736; fax (231) 943-7820
  zazattc@traverse.net

Web site design and hosting

- bookzone
  Mary Westheimer
  3260 N. Hayden Road, Ste. 101
  Scotsdale, AZ 85251
  (800) 536-6162
  www.bookzone.com
  Free on-line marketing information.

- Lucid Design
  Nina Tovish
  313 Wisconsin Ave., N.W., Ste. 216
  Washington, D.C. 20016
  (202) 537-6705
  ninatovish@luciddesign.com   www.luciddesign.com

- Mercury Grafx
  Lou Eisenman
  11 Stephens Road
  Buzzards Bay, MA 02532
  (508) 759-8484
  info@mercurygrafx.com   www.mercurygrafx.com
  Offers design and hosting.

- MuseArts
  Chris Grotke and Lise LePage
  41 Cedar St. #1
  Brattleboro, VT 05301
  (802) 254-0129; fax (802) 254-5726
  grotke@musearts.com   www.musearts.com
  Excellent animation and special effects. Outstanding design work and
  Web hosting. Finalist in French animation festival.

- PrecisionWeb Hosting
  2210 East Vista Way, Ste. 5
  Vista, CA 92084
  (760) 630-1188
  www.precisionweb.net
  Offers Web hosting and free shopping cart.

Wholesalers

- Baker & Taylor (Southern warehouse)
  251 Mount Olive Church Road
  Commerce, GA 30599
  (706) 335-5000; (800) 775-1100; fax (800) 775-7480
  www.btol.com

- Baker & Taylor (billing department and Midwest warehouse)
  501 S. Gladiolus St.
  Momence, IL 60954
  (815) 472-2444; (800) 775-2300; fax (800) 775-3500
  btinfo@baker-taylor.e-mail.com

- Baker & Taylor (buyers' offices and warehouse)
  50 Kirby Ave.
  Somerville, NJ 08876
  (908) 218-3944; fax (908) 218-3966
  emarket@btol.com

- the distributors
  702 S. Michigan St.
  South Bend, IN 46601
  (219) 232-8500; fax (312) 803-0887
  Actually a wholesaler. Takes books on consignment, pays well, and recycles returns when possible.

- Hervey's Booklink & Cookbook Warehouse
  P. O. Box 831870
  Richardson, TX 75083
  (214) 212-2711
  info@herveys.com   www.herveys.com

- Ingram Book Company
  Ericka Littles, new vendor titles
  One Ingram Blvd.
  Box 3006
  LaVergne, TN 37086-1986
  (615) 793-5000; (800) 937-8100; fax (615) 793-3823

Major Web bookstores

- Amazon.com
www.amazon.com
Amazon.com has two programs for authors and publishers. If you have
no Web site you should join Amazon's "Advantage" program. To
register, go to the home page and click on "Great Programs," then on
"Advantage," then "Books," and "Join." Fill out the form. If it is
accepted, Amazon will stock your book in its warehouse. If you have a
Web site you may be able to also join the "Associates" program where
you can link your site directly to Amazon.com, which will take and fill
the orders, then pay you a commission. In either program your book
must have an ISBN and a bar code.

- Barnes & Noble
www.bn.com
Also has a program where authors and publishers can submit their
books for approval and inclusion. Go to the home page and click on
"Publisher and Author Guide." Follow the directions and fill out the
necessary form. Again, your book must have proper credentials.

- Borders Books & Music
www.borders.com
Borders has entered into an arrangement with Amazon.com whereby
books on the Borders site are linked to Amazon's shopping cart.
Basically, Borders is one of Amazon's Associates.

Useful Web sites

- Acronyms/abbreviations
www.acronymfinder.com/

- American Booksellers Association.
www.BookSense.com

- American Society of Indexers
www.asindexing.org

- Area codes and Zip codes in the United States
www.areacodeszipcodes.com

- Ask a Librarian
www.loc.gov/rr/askalib/
An on-line library service from the Library of Congress and many
public libraries. Ask a question, get an answer within five days. Great
idea—we've used it!

- Bartlett's Quotations
  www.cc.columbia.edu/acis/bartleby/bartlett

- Bill Walsh's, author of *Lapsing into a Comma*, provides information for copy editors
  www.theslot.com

- Biographies
  www.isleuth.com/refe-bios.html

- Book signings and literary events distributed free to newspapers and Web sites. Additional services have fee. Authors provide information about upcoming events.   www.netread.com

- Britannica On-line
  www.eb.com

- *The Chicago Manual of Style* (Q&A)
  www.press.uchicago.edu/Misc/Chicago/cmosfaq.html

- Discount Book Clubs in the United Kingdom and Europe
  www.bookclubsuk.com

- *Elements of English Style* (1918)—William Strunk Jr.
  www.cc.columbia.edu/acis/bartleby/strunk

- Grammar Lady Mary Newton Bruder has a grammar hotline. You can talk to the Grammar Lady during the hours of 9:00 A.M. to 5:00 P.M. Eastern time, Monday through Friday at (800) 279-9708 mary@grammarlady.com   www.grammarlady.com

- How things work.
  www.howthingswork.com

- Information Please Dictionary
  www.infoplease.com/

- Internet publisher with vast resources on site, including dictionaries, style and reference books.
  www.bartleby.com

- Library of Congress
  Frequently asked questions:
  www.cweb.loc.gov/faq/catfaq.html#22

- Lloyd Rich, copyright attorney
  www.publaw.com   info@publaw.com
  Free on-line newsletter to publishing community concerning copyright, trademarks, contracts, and Internet law.

- Marketing and writing information by Judy Cullins, the "Book Coach"
  www.bookcoaching.com/

- *Merriam-Webster Collegiate Dictionary* on-line
  www.m-w.com/netdict.htm

- Merriam-Webster On-line Thesaurus
  www.m-w.com/mw/theslimt.htm

- Miss Abigail Time Warp Advice
  www.MissAbigail.com
  Her wonderful advice for contemporary problems is drawn from an extensive library of old books. Miss Abigail also links readers to bookstores specializing with old and out-of-print books.

- Multilingual On-line Dictionaries
  www.facstaff.bucknell.edu/rbeard/diction.html

- On-line Style Guide from Columbia University
  www.columbia.edu/cu/cup/cgos/odx_basic.html

- Pedro's Dictionaries—Multilingual dictionaries from Iowa State University
  www.public.iastate.edu/~pedro/dictionaries.html

- Thesaurus of Geographic Names
  http://www.getty.edu/research

- Indiana University—Plagiarism explanation
  www.indiana.edu/~wts/wts/plagiarism
  Anyone using material from other sources should read this excellent explanation of plagiarism.

- *Vocabula Review*, Robert Harwell Fiske, editor
  www.vocbula.com info@vocabula.com www.geographic.org
  A monthly journal about the state of the English language for $4.95. Fiske is author of *The Dictionary of Concise Writing*, and *The Dimwit's Dictionary* and offers an on-line writing and editing service.

- Words and vocabulary. An on-line English language journal.
  www.vocabula.com

- World Fact Book (1997)—CIA
  www.odci.gov/cia/publications/factbook/index.html

- World Fact Book
  www.geographic.org

Endnotes

Chapter 1

1. *Sarasota Herald-Tribune,* August 16, 1991.

2. *Publishers Weekly,* February 14, 1994.

3. Ibid., April 29, 1996.

4. *New York Times*, April 28, 1996.

5. Ibid., December 26, 1994.

6. *Publishers Weekly*, April 29, 1996.

7. Ibid., May 25, 1995.

8. *SPAN Connection*, Marilyn and Tom Ross, July 1996.

9. Publishers Marketing Association (PMA) newsletter March 1999.

Chapter 2

10. *U.S. News & World Report*, June 8, 1992.

Chapter 3

11. National Public Radio "All Things Considered," December 20, 1994.

12. *ForeWord* magazine, October 1999.

13. Lucia Staniels, publicist.

Chapter 4

14. *Aldus* magazine, July/August 1995.

Chapter 5

15. Florida Publishers Association meeting, March 1994.

16. *New Yorker* magazine, July 23, 2001.

17. *Wall Street Journal*, September 7, 1995.

Chapter 6

18. Paul Tulenko column *(Sarasota Herald-Tribune),* October 29, 2001.

Chapter 7

19. Associated Press *(Sarasota Herald-Tribune)*, August 3, 1996.

20. *PMA* newsletter, April 1999.

21. *New Yorker* magazine, "Science of the Sleeper," by Malcom Gladwell, October 4, 1999.

Chapter 8

22. Excerpted with permission from "Can online book publishing stop the (big) presses?" by Kim Campbell, *The Christian Science Monitor* July 24, 2000.

23. Marie Aloisi, vice president retail industries, *American Express Retail Strategies*, September 1999.

24. *St. Louis Post-Dispatch*, July 12, 1999.

25. Associated Press *(Sarasota Herald-Tribune)*, August 31, 1999.

26. *PMA Newsletter*, Judith Appelbaum, "POD Q&A," December 2001.

Chapter 9

27. *The Home Town Advantage: How to Defend Your Main Street Against Chain Stores . . . and Why It Matters* (Institute for Local Self-Reliance), p. 30.

Glossary

—A—

Acid-free paper: Neutral pH paper or alkaline paper, free from acid or other ingredients that destroy paper. Some libraries prefer acid-free paper, but it costs more. It's good for archival works and family histories—books that last and don't circulate much.

Adobe Acrobat: The computer program that converts document files into PostScript language (Distiller), then into PDF (Portable Document Format), or allows PDF documents to be viewed (Reader). Acrobat Reader is available as a free download from www.adobe.com.

Advance copies: Copies of book sent to a customer right after it comes off press but before the rest of the run is shipped.

Air: White space. This is the extra space between lines, left for margins or around artwork to keep the page from looking crowded or dark.

Align/alignment: To line up or position the print on a page with that on the adjacent page and on the reverse of the same page.

Appendix: Material in the back of the book that is related but not essential. Part of the "back matter." See *The Chicago Manual of Style* for how to set up the appendix and other parts of your book.

Art/artwork: Illustrations, photographs, drawings, paintings, and maps.

Author alterations (A.A.): These are changes made by the author during blueline proofing and are charged to the author/publisher.

Author/publisher: A self-publishing author who has applied for a bank of ISBNs and either set up the book himself or employed a packager to do the project.

Back flap: The back inside fold of a dust jacket, usually featuring a photo and biographical information of the author, and publisher's imprint.

Back lining: A strip of paper or fabric used to strengthen the spine of a casebound book.

Back matter: The selections at the back of the book including appendix, glossary, index, bibliography, and related material.

Bad break: Starting or ending a page with a widow or orphan or other awkward or messy look. May also refer to an inappropriate hyphenation in a word at the end of a line.

Bar code: A series of vertical bars encoded with the title, ISBN, and price of your book. Bookland EAN bar code should be printed at bottom of back cover.

Binder board: A stiff, high-grade composition board used in book binding. The cloth is glued over it to make the case or hard cover.

Bleed: An image or color that extends beyond the trim edge of the page, or from one page to another in a spread. Most book covers are designed to bleed, rather than have a border at the trim edge.

Bluelines (blues): Bluelines, like architectural drawings, are a photoprint made from stripped-up negatives or positives, used to check the position of the elements, and assuring that the pages are in order. They should not be used for a final proofing. Bluelines must be approved and returned quickly to keep book production on schedule.

Body copy: The primary part of the text.

Body text: Type used for the body copy. It may be different from that used for headings.

Boldface: The glossary words are set in **boldface** (b.f.) or a heavier face type to make them stand out.

Book block: The sewn and trimmed signatures which are ready to be bound. Everything put together but the cover.

Book cloth: The special cloth used for book covers. Like linens, the quality is determined by the number of threads per inch and their strength.

Book manufacturing: The specialized process of printing and binding the book.

Book packaging: A process by which a self-publishing author contracts to have a book professionally produced, receiving the entire press run.

Book style: Adhering to an accepted set of standard abbreviations, spellings, capitalizations, and punctuation. Use *The Chicago Manual of Style, The Associated Press Stylebook,* and a dictionary.

Bound galley: A copy of the finished book, uncorrected page proofs, or manuscript bound with a cheap cover and sent to those reviewers who want to see the book in advance of publication. Sometimes called "Cranes" after the company that originally produced them.

Browser: A software package such as *Netscape* or Microsoft *Explorer* that guides the user through the World Wide Web and displays HTML codes as text and graphics.

Bulk: The thickness of a book without the cover. Heavier papers can "bulk" up a book to make it thicker, sometimes important for thin volumes that must be a certain thickness if they are to be casebound.

—C—

C1S: Coated one side. Papers used for paperback book covers and dust jackets have an enamel coating on one side.

C2S: Coated two sides. Both sides of the paper used for paperback book covers are coated with enamel.

Camera-ready copy: An often misused term meaning the material ready for reproduction—the final copy going to the book manufacturer.

Casebound: Another name for hardcover.

Cataloging in Publication/CIP: Information for catalog card provided by the Library of Congress (after its review of the manuscript) or by some library distributors for inclusion on the copyright page.

CMYK: Cyan, magenta, yellow and black. The four colors of ink used to print full, four-color work.

Coated paper: Mineral and chemical substances, usually called enamel, that are applied to the paper to produce greater opacity or brightness. Can be either glossy or matte finish.

Coffee-table book: Large book with many illustrations, often with color photographs or prints, which is used for display.

Color key: An overlay proof composed of an individual colored acetate sheet for each of the PMS colors used by the printer. Used to check register, obvious blemishes, and size.

Color proof: A laser proof showing the approximate colors of the cover or artwork. Used to check for register or errors.

Copyright: Ownership of the work, protected by law. Copyright should be in name of owner—the author, publisher, or whoever paid for work.

Corner marks: Open parts of squares placed on original copy as a positioning guide. Shows the actual size of your book pages. Sometimes known as crop marks or printer's marks.

Crop/crop marks: To crop is to eliminate a part of a photograph or other illustration. Crop marks show the area to be saved, or to be eliminated.

Customer service rep (CSR): The service representative at the book manufacturer who is assigned to each project. Good reps will shepherd you and the book through the printing and binding process, facilitating production and schedules.

—D—

DPI: Dots per inch. The more dpi, the sharper the reproduction. Books should be printed at no less, and preferably more than 600 dpi for good quality reproduction.

Distributor: The middleman between the publisher and the retail outlet.

Drop ship: To ship an order to one address and bill charges to another.

Duotone: A two-color halftone reproduction from a one-color original.

Dust jacket: The printed paper cover wrapped around a casebound book. Also called a book jacket.

—E—

E-mail: Mail or messages sent electronically using the Internet. You need to be connected through a server before you can connect to others. An excellent method of keeping networking contacts alive.

EAN Bookland bar code: A series of vertical lines printed on the book's cover or jacket. The lines are encoded with price, ISBN, and title, and are scanned by computers for inventory and sales records.

Editor: Someone born with a red pen in hand who will help you breathe life into your material, assist with style, and check for accuracy.

EM dash or space: EM is a unit of measure in typesetting equal to the point size of the type in question. An em dash—is always used instead of a double hyphen--to indicate a change of thought in a sentence. There should be no space between the em dash and adjacent letters.

EN dash or space: Half the size of an em. Used instead of a hyphen to indicate range of dates or numbers, i.e. 1910–14.

Endsheets: Two pages of strong paper wrapped around the book block of a casebound book, with one leaf of each pasted to the inside board of the case. Can be plain or printed with colors and designs.

Extract: Section of material taken from another book or from another author, set in smaller type or indented.

—F—

F&G: Folded and gathered, not yet bound book block.

Fax: An inexpensive and speedy electronic means to send printed or written information, receive orders, and communicate via telephone circuits.

Facing pages: Two pages that face each other when the book is open.

Film lamination: A process of bonding plastic film on the cover to protect it from scratching and improve the appearance.

Font: Full assortment (upper and lower case, numerals, symbols, etc.) of a specific size and style of type.

Foreword: A statement by an expert (not the author) in the front matter. Do not confuse with "forward," which means to advance or move ahead.

Front flap: Usually features a synopsis or teaser about the content, the price, and ISBN.

Front matter: The front section (foreword, preface, introduction, etc.), with pages numbered in Roman numerals, that comes before the book body.

Fulfillment house: A place where orders, usually for single copies, are taken and books shipped. Will have credit card capability and will take 800 calls twenty-four hours a day.

—G—

Galley/galley proof: Typeset material before it has been formatted into book form.

GIF: Graphics Interchange File format for graphics on the Web.

Gutter: The blank space between columns of type or text and spine.

Gray scale: A scale of gradations of gray, from white to black. It measures the range and contrast of a scanned image.

—H—

Half-title page: Front matter page containing only the book title or section title, before the title page, used as the "autographing page."

Hard copy: The paper printout of what is on your computer screen.

Halftone: A photographic image that has been printed through a screen composed of minute dots. This breaks up the image so that it can be reproduced with proper contrast in the printing process.

Header: The headline at the beginning of a chapter (chapter head) or the beginning of a section (section head) or a new topic (subhead).

High contrast: The darkness between adjoining areas is well-defined, sometimes greater than in the original photograph.

Home page: The index or menu page of a Web site. The page that a user will be taken to first, and from which they can get to all parts of the Web site.

HTML: HyperText Markup Language. The coding language used to program Web sites.

—I—

Imprint: The identifying name of the publishing company, which is printed on the book.

Independent publisher: A publishing house that is not publicly owned or one of the Big Guys.

International Standard Book Number (ISBN): A number assigned to the publisher by R.R. Bowker that identifies each book. The ISBN should be printed on the copyright page, the back cover and spine.

Internet: A system of worldwide communication over telephone lines, cable, and satellite links that is available through Internet providers (usually local) or on-line services such as AmericaOnline or Comcast.

ISBN: See International Standard Book Number

Italic: Sloped letters. If needed for emphasis, *use sparingly!* Also used to mark titles of books and magazines in text.

—J—

JPG: A low-resolution file format used to place images on the World Wide Web. JPG is IBM; jpeg is MAC.

Justify: To have the text set flush left and/or right. The lines of text are squared off and the type is spaced to evenly fill the line. Most books are justified. This one, however, is justified on the left margin, but not the right.

—K—

Kerning: Adjusting the space between two characters for aesthetics, so they appear closer together, or farther apart. This word, fly, is not kerned. This one is: fly. Note the spaces between the "f" and the "l."

—L—

Layout: A working diagram of how the page(s) will look for artist, typesetter, or printer to follow as a guide.

Leaders:.............Rows of dots or dashes to guide the eye across the page. Use sparingly. Try to avoid using them in the table of contents.

Leading: The space between lines of type, measured from baseline to baseline and expressed in points.

Leaf: Each piece of paper in the book, with a page on each side.

Library binding: A stronger, heavily reinforced binding that meets the standards of the American Library Association.

Link(s): Hyperlinks. Those coded and highlighted words or icons in an HTML document that, when clicked, will transport a Web user to another page in a Web site or even to another site in the Web.

Long run: A print run in excess of 10,000 copies.

—M—

Marketing: Finding out what the public wants and meeting its needs. A self-publishing author's responsibility.

Mass-market paperback: Books produced inexpensively for distribution in supermarkets, drug stores and some bookstores. Usually small, approximately 4½ x 6 inches, and produced in quantity at low unit cost.

Match print: A photographic print of a four-color cover or page made from the film that the plates will be made from. Used by the pressman to check accuracy of the colors as they are printed.

Matte: Dull finish. No luster or gloss.

Mechanicals: Copy that uses overlays to indicate the position and register of each element or color to be printed. Color key.

Moisture content: A measure of relative humidity that expresses the amount of water in paper.

—N—

NAIP: National Association of Independent Publishers.

NAIPR: National Association of Independent Publishers Representatives.

Nocurl paper: A new process that keeps paperback covers from curling up in high humidity.

—O—

Offset lithography: A printing process in which image area and non-image area exist on same plate and are separated by chemical repulsion.

Orphan: The first line of a paragraph that is left at the bottom of a page. Orphans signal lack of professionalism in book formatting.

Otabind: One of several patented binding processes that adapt perfect binding so that it can lie flat without being held open.

Out of register: Pages on both sides of sheet or colors that are not aligned.

—P—

Page: One side of a leaf.

Page proof: Proof of type in page form. The final proofs before going to camera-ready.

Paperbound: Paperback or softcover book.

PDF: Portable Document Format. An electronic format produced by Adobe Acrobat that allows books to be sent to the printer as electronic files on disk or CD. PDF preserves the document's format yet is not memory intensive.

Perfect bound: A binding method that uses flexible adhesive to hold each page in place after folds along the spine have been cut off. Most paperback books are perfect bound.

Pick 'n Pack: A shipping house that will store and ship your books. You fax them your orders and they will pick, pack, and ship them for you. Some also have fulfillment services.

Plastic comb binding: Also called GBC binding after the company that originated the process. A type of binding made of rolled, rigid plastic cut in the shape of a comb or rake, and inserted through slots punched in the spine edge of the book pages. Cookbooks and workbooks are often bound this way.

PostScript: A computer language that allows much flexibility in the type of fonts and formatting of electronic files. Documents must be converted to PostScript before being distilled to PDF files.

PPI (pages per inch): The number of pages contained in one inch stack of paper. Varies depending on the weight of the paper.

Preface: Part of front matter and serves as introductory material.

Prelims: Preliminary pages or front matter.

Prepress: All the manufacturing setup work prior to going on the press. Includes photography, film and plate making, and registration of plates on the press.

Printer's error (P.E.): A necessary correction or change caused by an error by the printer and is not billed to the customer.

Print-on-demand: A method of printing used by publishers for short runs or single-copy orders. Books are created by a duplexing copy machine. Covers can be either printed or produced by copy process.

Process colors: Yellow, cyan blue, magenta red, and black. Thousands of colors can be produced using these colors in various combinations.

Publisher: The company or person whose ISBN is applied to the book, whose imprint appears on the title page, and who presents the literary product to the public.

Publisher's rep: A person who tries to sell your book to a distributor, wholesaler, or to the independent stores. See commission rep.

—R—

Ragged right: Type that is justified on the left margin and is unjustified on the right. This book's type is set ragged right.

Recto: A right-hand, odd-numbered page.

Resolution: The degree of sharpness in either a screen display or an image, measured in dots per inch. A low resolution (72 dpi) is used in newspaper printing and for computer screen images, while higher resolutions (300 or 600 dpi) are used in laser printers. Highest resolution (1200 to 2450 dpi) comes from laser typesetters and image setters or electronic press-ready PDF files.

Retail: Selling to the general public at the stated price of the product.

Roman type: A regular typeface, as opposed to italic or boldface versions of the same type.

Rules: Vertical or horizontal lines on a page.

Run: Press run. The number of copies printed in a single printing.

Running head: A headline or chapter title repeated at the top of each page, for quick reference of the reader.

Saddlestitch: A binding process that fastens the pages or signatures of a book together with wire stitches or staples through the middle fold.

Sans serif: A style of typeface that does not have serifs or ticks at the ends of letters. More difficult to read. Do not use for book text. However, sans serif can be used effectively for headers or subheads.

Screen: A network of crisscross lines of dots which break up a continuous tone image into a pattern that can be printed in black and white to represent gradations of gray. Without a screen your photographs will be reproduced as if by a copy machine. Used to make halftones.

Self-publisher: Realistic and courageous author who understands the reality of the publishing market, knows that a book is a product, and takes control of his or her destiny.

Serifs: Small extensions or ticks on the bases and tops of letters. They make the type easier to read because they lead the eye to the next letter. Serif fonts should be used for the body text of a book.

Service bureau: A company that specializes in support services for designers, printers, and photographers. Service bureaus do screening, halftones, color separations, proofs, and camera-ready output.

Sheet-fed press: A printing press that prints on individual sheets of paper. Each sheet is then folded and trimmed to make a signature. Most economical for short-run books.

Shrink-wrap: A clear plastic covering, heat shrunk to fit tightly around copies of your book. Helps protect books during shipping and from humidity. Sometimes enhances salability.

Signature: A part of a book consisting of a group of pages that has been folded and trimmed. There may be 4, 8, 16, 24, or 32 pages to the signature. Plan your book so that the page count comes out in even signatures.

Small press: An independent press. A small press can be a single-title author/publisher, or a rights-buying publisher.

Smart self-publisher: Someone who does it right!

Smyth-sewn: Signatures sewn together with thread by linked stitching on back of the fold and through the centerfold, permitting the binding to open almost flat, and strengthening the entire book block.

Spine: The back of a bound book connecting the two covers. Title, author's name, and sometimes publisher's imprint and/or ISBN are printed on it.

Stripping: Placing the various elements of the layout in their proper positions on the flats, which will be used to make the final plates.

Subsidy press: A publishing company that applies its ISBN to a book and charges the author for the cost of production. The author receives only a few copies of the book, and is promised royalties on those copies that might be sold by the subsidy press.

—T—

Tag: In HTML, the code that tells browser software to apply, or to stop applying, a certain type of style or format to a part of a document.

TIF: Tagged Image file, format for saving photos and scans for printing.

Title page: The page in a book's front matter, usually recto, which states the title, author, and publisher. Follows half-title page.

Trade paperback: The name given to the common softcover books sold in bookstores. Usually they are 6 by 9 or 5½ by 8½ inches in size and are printed on substantial paper. Not "mass market."

Trap: An area of overlapping ink where different colors of ink meet. Traps prevent unwanted white edges, where the paper color shows through, between areas of different colors.

Typeface: A style or design of type encompassing shape, weight, and proportions which make it distinct from other typefaces. Use a conventional typeface for your body text.

Typo: Another word for typographical error. Find them during the proofing process, not at blueline stage or after the book is in print.

—U —

Uncoated paper: Paper on which the printing surface consists of the paper stock itself. Usually used to print the body of the book. Books made with uncoated cover stock (card stock) usually look homemade.

Underlining: Don't use it for titles or emphasis in books. Use *italics*.

URL: Universal Resource Locator. The "address" of a site on the World Wide Web.

UV coating: A liquid protective coating applied to covers or dust jackets during the printing process that is dried by means of ultraviolet lights. Not as protective as film lamination, but better than varnish.

—V—

Vanity press: Another term for a subsidy press. It implies that the published book has no value other than to stroke the author's ego.

Varnish: A thin protective coating applied to a printed sheet or cover during the printing process. It provides protection and gloss for appearance; cheaper than lamination, but with less gloss and providing less protection.

Verso: A left-hand page of a book, properly an even-numbered page. *The* verso page contains the copyright and other important information.

—W—

Walk-around: A person dressed in costume who walks around at a mall or shopping center during a book signing to help promote a book.

Web: See World Wide Web.

Webmaster: A computer buff who is able to produce exceptionally striking art and format of pages on the World Wide Web.

Web press: A printing press that uses large rolls of paper rather than individual sheets. Economical for long print runs (more than 10,000 copies). Newspapers and magazines are printed on web presses.

Web page: A page on a Web site, usually the Home page, but any page if the site has more than one page.

Wholesale: A price given to re-sellers that reflects a discount from the stated retail price.

Widow: A short single line at the top of a page or column, usually the last line of the last paragraph from the preceding page; to be avoided in good typesetting. Also, a single word or syllable produced by a bad break standing alone as the last line of a paragraph.

World Wide Web: The network of personal and commercial information sites on the computer-served Internet. The World Wide Web is the host for individual Web sites, which consist of Home pages and other pages connected to the Home pages via hyperlinks.

Index

plans, 122
responsibility for, 51, 77–78, 159
Publisher's Cataloging in Publication
(PCIP), 59
Publisher's Graphics, 147
Publisher's rep, 134–35
Publishers Association of the South
(PAS), 154, 156
Publishers, major, xi, 1–4, 83, 102,
129, 157–58
Publishers Marketing Association
(PMA), 127, 134, 142, 151, 153,
156
Publishers, niche, 8, 50
Publishers, small, 3, 4
Publishers Weekly
on publishing industry, 2, 3, 7, 8,
77, 140
reviews, 78, 80, 81, 158
Publishing, changes in, 1–4, 139
Punctuation, 27, 28

Q

Quality, 8, 150–51
Quality Books, 129, 131
Quark Express, 74
QuickBooks, 112
Quicken, 112
Quoted material, permission for, 30–31

R

R. R. Bowker Company, 4, 55
*Radio and Television Interview Report
(RTIR)*, 98
Radio interviews, 97–100
Rainbow Books, Inc., ix, x, 107, 142
Rapid Descent, 136
Rawlings, Marjorie Kinnan, xv
Rawlinson, Nora, 2
Readers, determining, 25, 36, 41, 51,
78
Readers' theater, 105
Reciprocal links, 142, 143, 145
Record keeping, 111, 112–13

Recto page, 57, 64
Red Planet Blues, 100
Reed Reference Company, 4
Reference books, 25, 27
Reference lists, 65
Reference materials, 161–65
Regional books, 4, 37–38, 136
Regional distributors, 121, 135, 136
Regional newspapers, 93
Register of Copyrights, 58
Reilly, Patrick M., 101
Reprints, 147, 149
Resale certificate, 111
Researching markets, 35–36, 50, 78
Resolution of text, 74, 75
of photographs, 152
Resources, 167–98
Retail price, 46–48, 121, 159
Retail trade, 120, 121
Returns, 115, 125, 127–28
Reviews, 78–89, 101, 106, 158, 159
RGB format, 152
Riding the Bullet, 147
Rights, 9, 10
Road and Track Magazine, 87
Robertson, Anabel, 115
Robertson, Jim, 5, 93, 115
Roerden, Chris, 25
Roots, 39
Ross, Marilyn, 9
Ross, Tom, 9
Royalties, 1, 11
Running head, 65
Runs. *See* Press runs
Rust, Ann, 5

S

Sabah, Joe, 40, 100
Saddlestitch, 68
Sales
bookstores, 42
catalogs, 42
clubs, 6, 43
commissions, 121

About the authors

Courtesy Church Impressions

Linda and Jim Salisbury, award-winning publishers and book packagers, founded Tabby House in 1990. Her first book, *Good-bye Tomato, Hello Florida* published by Phoenix Press, was on the Southwest Florida best-seller list in the Fort Myers *News-Press* for several months. Her second book, Tabby House's first effort, *Read My Lips: No New Pets!*, brought an honorable mention in the National Association of Independent Publishers (NAIP) new book contest.

Linda was graduated from Oberlin College with a B.A. in English. She is an community news editor and columnist for a major Florida newspaper, and has had extensive experience in marketing and public relations. She is also a book reviewer.

Jim, a graduate of Upsala College with a B.S. in geology, spent many years teaching upper and middle school science, in retail sales and in real estate. He has served as president of the Florida Publishers Association and remains an advisor to the board of directors.

In addition to publishing their own books and providing book-packaging services to self-publishing authors, Jim and Linda often present seminars titled "Self-Publishing—The Last (or First) Resort" to writer's groups and others interested in learning about publishing their own books. *Smart Self-publishing* is an outgrowth of the many questions asked at those seminars, and the authors' many varied experiences in the publishing industry.

Tabby House is a member of the National Association of Independent Publishers (NAIP), the Publishers Association of the South (PAS), the Small Press Center, Publishers Marketing Association (PMA), Small Publishers Association of North America (SPAN), the Southeast Booksellers Association (SEBA) and the Florida Publishers Association (FPA).

Acknowledgments

We appreciate the suggestions and comments of the many individuals who are quoted by permission in this book. Some are authors for whom we have packaged books; many others are not. Some are book professionals who have written segments about their areas of expertise: Alex Moore, Chris Roerden, Mary Westheimer, Lise LePage, Sandi Frank, Denny Fried, Giles Hoover, Betty Wright and Joe Sabah.

We are grateful to the self-publishing authors, and others, who have read various drafts of *Smart Self-Publishing* and shared their thoughts, experiences, and red proofing pens. And we appreciate the encouragement of those who buy and distribute books and the support we have received from our fellow publishers. Most of all, we have enjoyed hearing from the many people around the country who have found each edition helpful as they contemplated or worked on their book projects.

We are especially thankful for the talents of Christopher Grotke, who created the graphics, and Abigail Grotke for the initial book design.